MAU'I
Mile by Mile
2nd Edition

Researched, Written, & Photographed by:

John Derrick
Natasha Derrick

HAWAIIAN
STYLE

Hawaiian Style Organization LLC
www.HawaiianStyle.org

MAU'I - MILE BY MILE; Second Edition

Published by:
Hawaiian Style Organization LLC
PO BOX 965
Columbia, South Carolina 29202-0965
www.HawaiianStyle.org

Published 2006
ISBN 0-9773880-5-0
Library of Congress Control Number: 2005910121
Printed in the United States

A special mahalo (thanks) to our proofreaders:
Dot Derrick and Amanda Taylor

Language Note: Hawai'i's two official languages are Hawaiian and English, the only state in the US with two official languages. In this guide we have attempted to use both the English and Hawaiian names of places when possible. There are only 13 letters in the Hawaiian alphabet: A, E, H, I K, L, M, N, O, P, U, W and the 'okina ('). The okina is a glottal stop like the sound between the ohs in "oh-oh" and is considered a consonant. In order to clarify pronunciation, you will often see the glottal stop (') or 'okina used on words in this guide such as Hawai'i. Due to printing restrictions, we will not use the macron, which is found above stressed vowels in the Hawaiian language. Crash course in pronunciation below:

The vowels are pronounced:
A as in father, E as in vein, I as "ee" in peep, O as on own, and U as "oo" in boo.

The consonants are pronounced:
H as in hale, K as in Kate, L as in laid, M as in moon, N as in noon, P as in peak, and W as in always.

All photographs (except satellite imagery and where otherwise noted) taken by John and Natasha Derrick. Satellite imagery courtesy of NASA.

TABLE OF CONTENTS

Introduction   i

Overview of Mau'i, Hawai'i   ii

Mau'i by Region   iii

      -West Mau'i   iii

      -South Mau'i   iv

      -Central Mau'i   v

      -Upcountry Mau'i   vi

      -East Mau'i   vii

Synopsis of our Guide   viii

The Demi-God Mau'i   xi

The Road to Hana

1

Map of the Road to Hana (Mile Markers 1-20)   3

1.) Starting Point - Pa'ia Town   4

2.) Ho'okipa Beach Park   5

3.) Highway 360 to Highway 31   6

4.) Twin Falls Trail   7

5.) Painted Bark Eucalyptus Trees   8

6.) Waikamoi Ridge Trail & Overlook   9

7.) Garden of Eden Botanical Arboretum   12

8.) Lower & Upper Puohokamoa Falls   14

9.) Haipua'ena Falls   16

10.) Kaumahina State Wayside Park   17

11.) Honomanu Bay Lookout   18

12.) Punalau Valley Falls   19

13.) Honomanu Bay Road   20

14.) Road to Hana Highway Lookouts   21

TABLE OF CONTENTS

15.) Nua'ailua Bay & Scenic Lookout — 23
16.) Keanae Arboretum & Garden — 24
17.) Keanae Peninsula & Village — 26
18.) Ching's Pond (Sapphire Pools) — 27
19.) Keanae Peninsula Lookout — 28
20.) Wailua Valley Wayside Park — 29
21.) Waikani (Three Bears) Falls — 30
Map of the Road to Hana (Mile Markers 19-34) — 31
22.) Pua'a Ka'a State Wayside Park — 32
23.) Lava Tubes & Caves — 33
24.) Hanawi Falls — 34
25.) Makapipi Falls — 35
26.) Nahiku Road & Landing — 36
27.) Pi'ilani Heiau & Kahanu Garden — 38
28.) Blue Angel Falls & Blue Pool (KAPU) — 39
29.) Wai'anapanapa Wayside Park — 40
30.) Hana Town, Bay, & Ranch — 42

Beyond Hana Town
45

Beyond Hana Maps (Mile Markers 51-38) — 46
1.) Starting Point - Hana Town — 47
2.) Haneo'o Road & Ancient Fishponds — 49
3.) Koki Beach & Alau Island — 50
4.) Hamoa Beach — 52
5.) Venus Pool — 54
6.) Wailua Falls — 56

7.) Ohe'o Gulch (Seven Sacred Pools) 58
-Kipahulu Area Hiking Guide 60
8.) Pipiwai Trail 61
9.) Makahiku & Waimoku Falls 62
10.) Charles Lindbergh's Grave 64
11.) The Rough & Bumpy Road 66
12.) Alelele Trail & Falls 68
13.) Mokulau & Kaupo Store 69
14.) Kaupo Gap Lookout 70
15.) Pokowai Sea Arch 71
16.) Highway 31 Gulch 72
17.) Tedeschi Winery & Ranch Store 73
18.) Sun Yat-Sen Memorial Park 74
19.) Highway 37 & 377 (Junction 1) 75
20.) Enchanting Floral Gardens 76
21.) Highway 37 & 377 (Junction 2) 77
22.) Highway 378 (Crater Road) Turn Off 78
23.) Kula Botanical Gardens 79
24.) Polipoli Springs State Park 80

Haleakala Highway
81

The Geology of Haleakala Volcano 83
1.) Starting Point - Haleakala Hwy 86
2.) Haleakala Highway Lookouts 88
3.) Haleakala National Park Entrance 90
Haleakala National Park Flora & Fauna 91
4.) Hosmer Grove Hike & Supply Trail 92

TABLE OF CONTENTS

5.) Park Headquarters Visitor Center 94
6.) Halemau'u Trailhead (To Summit) 95
7.) Leleiwi Overlook & Hike 96
8.) Kalahaku Overlook & Hike 98
9.) House of the Sun Visitor Center 100
10.) Haleakala Summit (Pu'u Ula'ula) 102
Haleakala Summit Activities 104
   -Hiking & Trail Guide 105
      -Pa Kaoao Trail 105
      -Sliding Sands Trail 106
      -Halemau'u Trail 109
   -Bike Riding 110
   -Horseback Riding (Into Crater) 112
   -Haleakala Sunrise Information 113

Other Mau'i
'Must See & Do'
115

La Perouse Bay 116
Makena Beach (Big Beach) 117
'Iao Valley & Needle 118
Dragon's Teeth 119
Kahekili Beach 120
Lahaina Town 121
Waihe'e Ridge Trail & Valley 122
Nakalele Blowhole 124

End Notes 125
Index 131

M<small>A U</small> I
Mile by Mile

INTRODUCTION

Mau'i is renowned worldwide for many things; its beauty, its atmosphere, its history, and its never ending supply of pristine beaches, waterfalls, landmarks, and gardens - just to name a few. There aren't a whole lot of places in the world you can  go and experience all you can on the small island of Mau'i, Hawai'i. What's more, is the fact you can access nearly all of Mau'i by vehicle. The roads literally skirt the edge of Mau'i's coastline all the way around, figuratively speaking in a large sideways "8" shape with each circle of the eight a mountainous volcanic landform. On the west side of the island stand the West Mau'i Mountains and on the east the tall, majestic, and expansive Mount Haleakala. Between the two you have the isthmus valley that famously dubs Mau'i the "Valley Isle."

This guidebook is designed to take you along the three most popular journeys on Mau'i. Whether you choose to view everything from your car seat or decide to head out into the grander scheme of things on foot, our guide is here to help you navigate the paths ahead of you. Each of the three major journeys can be done in a single day, so you can expect the core of our guide to fill a good three to four days of your time on Mau'i. Our additional section of Mau'i 'Must See & Do' can add several additional days of sightseeing and adventure to your trip. And since our details are precise, down to the mile, and our ratings based on good instinct, you can decide for yourself in good conscience which stops are for you and which aren't long before your own journey.

M A U I
Mile by Mile

We know your time on Mau'i is precious, and we understand you don't want to waste your time on certain spots or activities. So we'll always be completely straightforward with you on our thoughts about each spot. Ultimately, you're the travel planner for your visit to Mau'i, and by using our guide hopefully you too can have a wonderful experience in paradise.

OVERVIEW OF MAU'I, HAWAII

Mau'i is the second largest landmass in the Hawaiian island chain that consists of eight major islands and 124 islets. The archipelago is made up of numerous volcanic islands in the central Pacific Ocean stretching in a 1,500-mile crescent from Kure Island in the northwest to the Big Island of Hawai'i in the east, encompassing an area of 6,459 square miles. The eight major islands at the eastern end of the chain are, from west to east, Ni'ihau, Kaua'i, Oahu, Moloka'i, Lana'i, Kaho'olawe, Mau'i, and the Big Island of Hawai'i.

Our journey begins on the island of Mau'i. Mau'i is composed of two major volcanic areas, the older and extinct West Mau'i Mountains and a very expansive volcano named Haleakala on the eastern side of Mau'i. In between the two is a valley filled with deposits. In addition to these three primary areas, the island can be divided into several official sub-areas, and it's a good idea to become familiar with each of them. No area is quite like another on Mau'i.

MAUʻI BY REGION

• **West Mauʻi:** With plenty of sunshine and an abundance of rainfall (as much as 390 inches a year), West Mauʻi was once a major Hawaiian population center and the proverbial playground of royalty (the aliʼi) in old Hawaiʻi. Today, West

Mauʻi has become the playground of visitors from around the world. You'll now find the resort areas of Kapalua and Kaʼanapali; visitor communities of Napili, Kahana and Honokowai; and historic Lahaina town gracing the shores of West Mauʻi.

The mountains of West Mauʻi are some of the oldest volcanic features on the island at around one million years old.

iv

M_{Mile by Mile}AUI

• South Mau'i:

South Mau'i is best known for its miles of white sandy beaches, spectacular coastal areas, snorkeling on its reefs, and expansive lava fields like La Perouse Bay. Sheltered on the leeward side of Haleakala volcano, this

side of Mau'i is quite drier and sunnier than the rest of the island. Today, South Mau'i includes the coastal communities of Ma'alaea and Kihei and the growing resort communities of Wailea and Makena.

Lava fields like La Perouse Bay in South Mau'i offer an excellent chance for you to experience a recent, geologically speaking, lava flow up close and personal.

M A U I
Mile by Mile

• **Central Mauʻi:**
The proverbial "heart" of Mauʻi, Central Mauʻi, is the isthmus that connects Mauʻi's two volcanoes. Today, Central Mauʻi includes residential communities, sugar and pineapple plantations, county and state government

offices, and various visitor attractions including the famous ʻIao Valley & Needle, the Mauʻi Tropical Plantation, golf courses, parks, shopping areas, and more. Your visit to Mauʻi likely began here at the airport in Kahului.

Central Mauʻi is the proverbial heart of the island. Here you'll find Kahului airport and expansive sugar cane farmland.

M A U I
Mile by Mile

• Upcountry Mau'i:
"Upcountry Mau'i" re-
fers to the towns, ranch-
es, vineyards, parks,
farmlands, and visitor
attractions on the upper
slopes of Haleakala, in-
cluding Haleakala Na-
tional Park. Enchanting
and rural, the Upcoun-
try of Mau'i is the heart

of the island's agricultural industry as well as a thriving art-
ists' community. Many compare the beautiful landscape of
Upcountry Mau'i to the countryside in Scotland. You'll also
be sure to discover several unique floral gardens in this part
of Mau'i. Plus, some of the best views of the South Pacific
anywhere on the island can be found from the high elevations of the upcountry.

*This NASA photograph of Haleakala's summit shows just how
expansive the mighty crater basin really is.*

• East Mau'i:

East Mau'i ranges from Kahului Airport to the community of Hana (Haa-na) on the northeastern tip of the island and is renowned for great wind surfing, lush rural scenery, and, of course, the famous Road to Hana. Known

often as the windward side, it is largely undeveloped and much of the narrow Road to Hana winds along the island's beautiful northern coastline.

The appropriately named 'Garden of Eden' along the Road to Hana is but one of the many beautiful locations along East Mau'i. Here you can see the famous "Jurassic Park" rock.

MAUI
Mile by Mile

SYNOPSIS OF OUR GUIDE

In our guide we'll embark first on a tour of the Road to Hana, famous for its stunning coastal views, winding curves, one lane bridges, and never ending beauty along Mau'i's north east coast. There are many who will proclaim it to be the best drive in all of Hawai'i, and quite frankly, we're inclined to agree with them. And with the Road to Hana, it's not about how fast you can get to Hana Town, so take your time - slow down to the island's leisurely pace for a day. After all, it's the journey, not the destination that is the attraction with the Hana Highway. It's a journey and a drive that is truly magical and should be experienced by all. If there was ever a highway to heaven, then this would be it.

After driving to Hana Town you're not going to want to stop there, some of the best sights in all of Mau'i, and even Hawai'i, lie beyond on the eastern coast of Mau'i. The drive beyond Hana is often over-scrutinized by car rental companies. Pish-posh! We'll set the record straight. To not drive

this part of Mau'i would be one of the biggest mistakes of your vacation. The beauty of the Ohe'o Gulch and Kipahulu area is like no other place on earth. So, if you can handle 400-foot waterfalls, beautiful coastal scenery, and one of the world's top beaches, then you might just want to keep this drive on your itinerary. Don't let anyone talk you out of this amazing drive. The Beyond Hana drive ends with a visit to the upcountry in the heart of Mau'i.

Finally, we'll conclude with a visit to the altar of the sun, quite literally. Starting in upcountry Mau'i, we'll take you to the very top of Mount Haleakala, a 10,023 dormant volcano that will surprise and amaze you with activities and sights beyond your wildest dreams. From coasting downhill on a bike for 38 miles, to hiking inside one of the world's largest volcanic craters, Haleakala is sure to be a treat for all. We'll explore the mountain from top to bottom, showing you the gems of this ancient volcano.

We also feel it is important that you know our guidebook is written, researched, and photographed by us, the authors. We have made many trips up and down the roads in our guide to make sure we bring you the best possible details available for your own drive on these majestic journeys. Here's what we will present you with in our guide:

• **Place Ratings:** Each spot has a rating (1-5 stars; 5 best). None of our ratings have been influenced by anyone or anything other than what you will see/experience at each spot. If we liked the place, we'll tell you we liked it, and if we didn't, you're going to know about that too. Candor is better than embellishment in our opinion; so you'll know what to expect at each spot. Here's a look at the ratings:

☆☆☆☆☆ - Avoid

★☆☆☆☆ - Poor

★★☆☆☆ - So-So

★★★☆☆ - Good

★★★★☆ - Excellent

★★★★★ - Must See

M A U I
Mile by Mile

• **Photographs:** Our guide attempts to include a photograph of every major stop on each drive. In fact, we include so many photographs we can even use the term "fully-illustrated" on our cover. Plus, there is no fancy camera work or tricks with our guide's photos. The main difference between our photos and what you might see are the weather factors and/ or seasonal changes (i.e. - waterfall flow rates).

• **Mile markers:** Mile markers on Mauʻi are an interesting thing. Sometimes they exist and sometimes they don't, literally. We have strenuously attempted to keep these as accurate as possible, but given the unpredictability of some mile marker locations, combined with the fact they sometimes "grow legs," it's not a bad idea to use the odometer as a general guide while driving along each route.

So are your travel buds watering yet? If so, you're ready to hit the road and explore what is arguably the best island in the world. So let's take a journey, a trip to paradise, and let's do it *Hawaiian Style...*

MAUI
Mile by Mile

THE DEMI-GOD MAU'I

Legend has it that centuries ago there was born the demi-god named Mau'i. The heavens were held by his father, the netherworld by his mother. Mau'i was said to be the smallest of the family, but what he  lacked in size he made up for by being the quickest of mind. Mau'i also was known to be adventurous if not mischievous. Legend states how Mau'i was not the best when it came to fishing either, something his brothers excelled at and teased him about due to his lack of success.

Mau'i, in revenge, would sometimes use his wiliness to fill his boat with his brothers' fish. He would pull his boat close enough to his brother's so that when they got a fish he could distract them and use his line to snag their fish. At first, Mau'i's brothers were in awe of his ability but eventually they caught on and refused to take him fishing. Seeing that her son was very upset, Mau'i's mom sent him to his father to get a magic fish hook. She said,

"Go to your father. There you will receive the hook called Manaiakalani, the hook fastened to the heavens. When the hook catches land, it will raise the old seas together."

So Mau'i went to his father and returned with the hook and asked his brothers to let him join in another fishing expedition. They laughed at him and threw him off the boat – but they returned with no catch. Mau'i scolded them, saying that if they had allowed him to join in on the fishing, they would have more success. So, figuring they had nothing to lose, the brothers allowed Mauʻi to join them in their canoe for another chance. They paddled far from the aina (land) and threw their hooks into the sea. To their dismay, they only were able to catch sharks. The brothers mocked Mauʻi asking "Where are the fish you promised, our brother?"

So Mauʻi, confident with his magic hook, rose and threw it into the ocean. He chanted a power prayer and commanded the hook to catch the Great Fish below. The ocean began to move, the waves chopped at the boat, and swells rose up around them. Mauʻi quickly instructed his brothers to paddle with all their might and not look back. For two whole days Mauʻi held the line tight, his brothers all the while paddling as furiously as they could. Suddenly from below the depths of the ocean arose the tops of great mountains in a series of peaks that broke the surface of the ocean. Mauʻi shouted for his brothers to paddle harder and not look back while he pulled against the line and forced the peak's even farther out of the water. But alas, one of his brothers couldn't resist, he had to look. And as he gazed back in awe at the sight before Mauʻi's hook he dropped his paddle, the line began to slacken, and before he could call out to his brothers, the line snapped and the magic hook was lost forever beneath the sea.

Mauʻi shouted at his brothers,

"I had endeavored to raise a great continent but because of your weakness I have only these islands to show for all my efforts."

And today we find the Hawaiian Islands just as Mauʻi left them those long, long years ago.

Mauʻi's adventures did not stop with the magic hook however. After raising the islands from the sea Mauʻi settled with his mother, Hina, in the town of Hana on Mauʻi. There she worked on her tapa cloth, frustrated at how the cloth never could dry in the short hours of the day.

So, Mauʻi set off on a quest to strike a deal with La, the sun. La had been being lazy, always in a rush to get back to bed. Mauʻi had noticed that La always rose off the rim of Haleakala Crater, so Mauʻi climbed to the top of Mount Haleakala, weaved a rope using some strong ieʻie vines, and as La raced across the sky Mauʻi snared him down from the Kaupo Gap on Haleakala summit.

Mauʻi made a deal with La for him to "walk" more slowly and steadily across the sky each day, a little faster in the winter, a little slower in the summer. And thus today we can thank Mauʻi for our present length of daylight hours.

As if the Road to Hana wasn't beautiful enough already, the amazing variety of flowering plants will make the drive even more worth your while.

THE ROAD TO HANA

Highway to Heaven? It's close my friends. Aloha to the Road to Hana on the island of Mau'i, Hawai'i. When it comes to driving to Hana Town, it's the journey getting there, not the destination, that is the main attrac-

tion. As you drive along the 52 miles of undeveloped road, which has 56 one-lane bridges and 617 curves and turns, you will pass by the most breath-taking scenery on the face of the earth. It was literally a million years in the making.

While you'll have to get up early to start this trip (sunrise-7am) you'll find that earlier means less traffic, and the more traffic you can avoid the more enjoyable your trip down the highway will be. If there is one complaint about the Road to Hana, it's almost always about the traffic. So, avoid the rush, get started early, and you'll enjoy your trip significantly more.

Without any stops, it can take up to three hours to make the 52-mile journey to Hana. As you'll quickly learn, some locals will try and do it in half that time. Don't let yourself be rushed down the highway. You know you aren't making the straight drive and will be driving slower than average, so just be sure to pull over occasionally and let those by who are in a hurry.

All in all, you can expect your journey driving the Road to Hana to last about a day. It'll really depend on how much of a nature lover you are. We'll talk more on that in a bit.

There are very few stores or restaurants on this journey, and the prices keep getting higher the further down the road you go. There are several charming roadside stands selling refreshing tropical fruit, snacks and beautiful island flowers along the journey, but please remember that you can't take the fruit or the flowers out of Hawai'i, so only buy what you plan to enjoy while in the islands. We recommend picking up a foam cooler, ice, canned beverages, and some snacks/small meals before heading out. It is also good to bring along tissue in case the rest stops are out of toilet paper. You'll also want some rain gear and the sunblock (UV index is normally 12 to 14+ in Hawai'i). Bring your camera and plenty of film (or the digital camera), as you are sure to discover many amazing photo opportunities. Bring bottled water and proper footwear if you plan to hike any of the many stunning trails. A collapsible hiking pole isn't a half-bad idea either for some of the hikes, 3 or 4 'legs' are better than two. Trust us on that, we've lived and learned.

MAP OF THE ROAD TO HANA
Mile Markers 1 - 20

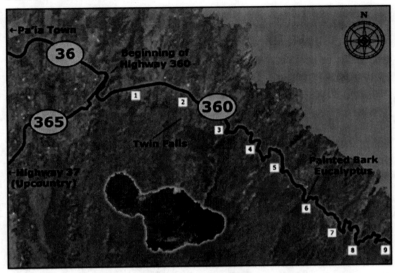

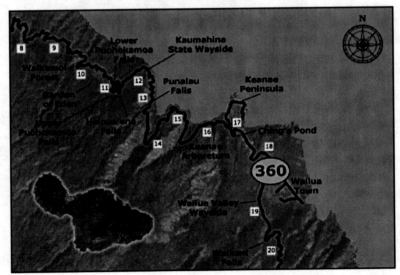

Map continues on page 31...

ROAD TO HANA

1.) STARTING POINT - PA'IA TOWN
Mile Marker 6 - Highway 36 (★★★☆☆)

The journey along the Road to Hana begins at a small town on Mau'i's north shore named Pa'ia (Pah-ee-ah) town. To get to Pa'ia town from the Kahului Airport, follow Highway 37 going southeast. Turn left onto Highway 365. Turn right onto Highway 36 and follow to it to where you enter Pa'ia town.

Pa'ia town is famous primarily for Ho'okipa Beach Park located right beyond the town to the left (our next stop). World-class windsurfing events are held here annually. Depending on when you travel, you'll likely see some surfers and/ or windsurfers in action. Historically speaking, Pa'ia was a sugar plantation town in the early 1900s.

If you haven't already, we highly suggest you fuel up your vehicle here. It's the last gas stop until Hana Town. It may also be a good place to grab a bite to eat for a picnic lunch later on the drive. Pa'ia also has some decent shopping considering its fairly small size, so you might even want to browse through some of the local shops. Some would argue that Pa'ia shops are superior to Lahaina stores on the west coast of Mau'i.

Once you've seen Pa'ia to your satisfaction, get back onto Highway 36 and head towards the junction of Hwy 36/360.

2.) HO'OKIPA BEACH PARK
Mile Marker 8 - Highway 36 (★★☆☆☆)

As we mentioned a moment ago, Ho'okipa Beach Park is located right beyond Pa'ia town, off to the left. You'll pass the steeply graded exit before you pass the entrance, so be looking for the sign marking the spot. There are two very different spots (hangouts) located inside small Ho'okipa

Beach Park: one is an overlook that is almost immediately to your right once you turn into the Park, and the other is the road that leads down to Ho'okipa Beach itself and then back up to the exit you passed prior to turning into the park at the sign. Ho'okipa Lookout is a nice spot to stop to get a good view over parts of coastal north west Mau'i (to your left) and the Pacific Ocean stretching to the north in front of you. It's also a great place to watch surfers catch the waves below you on Ho'okipa Beach. And after you're done at the lookout, your best bet is to get back on Highway 36 and continue your journey. You don't want to waste too much time at this location. Also the beach is a surfer's hangout, so the crowd is not always as full of "aloha" as people in other parts of Mau'i. We've never had any problems, but there are better beaches on Mau'i than this one, so why waste your time here? The real journey is still ahead of you.

3.) HIGHWAY 360 TO HIGHWAY 31
Mile Marker 0 - Reset Odometer (★☆☆☆☆)

As you continue down Highway 36 you'll eventually come to a location where the highway signs will change from Highway 36 to Highway 360. Be sure to start your odometer at 0 exactly at this spot.

Your journey will now begin down the Road to Hana along Highway 360. When you reach Hana Town the road will change into Highway 31. At this point you are better off by either staying in Hana Town for the night or turning around and making the trip back before dark instead of continuing on. The journey that begins just on the other side of Hana Town (the start of Highway 31) is another adventure in itself, and it too has some of the most amazing sites on Mau'i (some of our personal favorites actually). More on Highway 31 later, now let's go explore the Road to Hana.

4.) TWIN FALLS & TRAIL
Mile Marker 2 - Highway 360 (★★☆☆☆)

After you go through the intersection where the Highway to Hana begins you'll continue down the road until you go past mile marker 2. Here a bridge crosses the Hoʻolawanui stream and is where you'll find our first stop, but first a word of advice. Twin Falls is a very pretty place but compared to what is ahead of you, it's really just not worth the time or effort to stop here this early in your journey. We recommend either coming back to it later (on your way back out of Hana, etc), or just skipping it altogether. It's really up to you. We have talked with several people who have stopped at this location expecting grand waterfalls they'll never find until further down the road.

OK, so if you DO decide to stop, you can pull off and park on the right side of the road in a small parking lot which is usually accompanied by fruit stands. You may have to jump the fence to get on the trail (it takes some people a few minutes to figure that out) OR you can just walk through the open gate (recently, during our last visit, the gate has been open for all visitors). After you get beyond the fence you can walk through the small grassy area to a rock with a map drawn on it. Using this make-shift map you should be able to navigate to the various falls at this location. Once you park your vehicle and begin to hike, the round trip takes about 1 hour (including swimming time).

5.) PAINTED BARK EUCALYPTUS TREES
Mile Marker 6 - Highway 360 (★★★☆☆)

As we continue our journey beyond Twin Falls we'll head down the road until we reach about 6/10 mile past marker 6. Here you'll find some Painted Bark Eucalyptus trees off to the left in a small grove. These trees have a unique

bark that appears to have been hand-painted shades of red, purple and green. This location is not really a stop per se, as there really isn't much room to pull over. You have to kind of slow down and gaze at them. If you get on the highway early enough, you can probably even snap a few photos, like we did, without having to worry about any traffic jamming up behind you.

You can also get a glimpse of these trees at Keanae Arboretum, one of the stops that will come later in our journey down the Hana Highway. Pictures just can't capture the unique beauty of these trees.

We should also note that between this spot and our next stop you might notice a small waterfall off to your right. It's unnamed and nothing about it really warrants a stop, but most people don't know that and stop anyway. There are much better waterfalls down the road.

6.) WAIKAMOI RIDGE TRAIL & OVERLOOK
Mile Marker 9 - Highway 360 (★★★★★)

If lush tropical scenery is on the visual menu for the day then Waikamoi Forest is definitely your main course.

About 6/10 mile past mile marker 9 on the Hana Highway, keep your eyes open for the parking lot (on the right) to the Waikamoi Ridge Forest Trail and Overlook. It can be easy to miss due to the fact it's around a bend in the road, but make sure you don't miss it. After parking in the often crowded lot, head up to the open area to your left and you'll find a small overlook with picnic shelters and the Waikamoi trailhead.

The Waikamoi Trail is a beautiful, short nature walk through trees, bamboo and ferns, with scenic overlooks at various points along the way. There are actually two sections to the trail: one being a short loop that takes about half an hour and ends where it starts (at the picnic area) and the other a one-way extension from the loop trail. Both trails start at the picnic shelter located near the parking area. When starting the trail(s), we recommend you take the right path at the trailhead. It will take you counter clockwise around the loop and is ultimately an easier hike in that direction. When you get about half way along the loop trail (and at the first lookout bench) you'll notice the extension branching off to the right. This extension is well worth the extra effort because it's always less crowded than the loop trail and will take you further up the ridge. At the top of this ridge the trail breaks out of the trees into a grassy clearing with another shelter and picnic site. This overlook offers some really remarkable views of the highway. After you turn to head back, you'll return to the loop trail and take a right onto it. From there the loop-trail goes down the ridge to another bench overlook and then along the contour to the beginning point at the trailhead. And even if you decide to skip the extension, the loop trail is still a treat.

The trail is usually in good condition and hiking boots are not normally necessary. However, conditions can change with just one good rainstorm. The worst part of the loop-trail (when heading counterclockwise) is the part beyond

the extension trail. It goes steeply downhill at times and can be filled with roots. We suspect this will be "fixed" in the future, as volunteer groups have already improved the first half of the loop (as of summer 2005).

There is no water or restroom facility at this site, and we do recommend bug spray because the mosquitoes occasionally like to call this place home.

If you've never walked through a rainforest, this will be a real treat for you. It's a unique experience that we highly recommend. The Waikamoi Trail is a total of 0.8 miles if you do the loop-trail alone and about a mile and a half if you do the extension. Although it is short, it's one of the best trails on Mau'i. You can expect to spend about 30 minutes to an hour here if you do the short loop, and as many as 2 hours if you do one of the longer loops and/or have a picnic.

Waikamoi is mother nature at her finest. You won't get lost in Waikamoi Forest, but you might lose your everyday worries.

7.) GARDEN OF EDEN BOTANICAL ARBORETUM
Mile Marker 10 - Highway 360 (★★★★★)

At mile marker 10.5, off to the right (mauka or mountain) side of the road, you'll find The Garden of Eden Arboretum & Botanical Garden. This is another easy spot to miss, but make sure you make the stop. It'll likely be one of your favorites. Before you reach the garden there is a small sign to the right stating "Garden Next Right."

The garden is most popular for its debut in "Jurassic Park," where the opening sequence of the movie was filmed, specifically the "Jurassic Park Rock" which can be seen from one absolutely gorgeous lookout inside the garden.

The most amazing and beautiful coastal scenery in perhaps all of Mau'i is from the overlooks of this garden. The pristine white benches that are scattered around the grounds add just the perfect touch to this truly remarkable spot.

The 25-acre site was purchased in 1991 with a vision of restoring the area's natural ecosystem with Hawai'i's native and indigenous species. Along the way the opportunity arose to include exotic plants and trees from the South Pacific region and tropical rain forests throughout the world. Today there are over 500 botanically labeled plants, including the most extensive collection of Ti plants in Hawai'i. Ti has a long history of usage by the Polynesians in ceremonies and rituals and is still considered one of Hawai'i's most culturally useful plants. Many people stateside today also grow and love the Ti for its lore of being a "good luck plant." You can also catch a pretty good look at upper Puohokamoa Falls (our next stop) from this location. There are also several animals inside the gardens including peafowl, chickens, ducks, geese, and even some horses. If you're lucky you might also run into Bud 'The Birdman' Clifton at the exit of the garden. Bud and his famous parrots have traveled around the world, and you too will discover why they are famous if you stop in and say "hello."

Expect to spend about an hour or two at this location.

There is an admission charge of $10.00/per person as of this printing, but it is well worth it. The garden is open daily from 8:00 a.m. to 3:00 p.m. A good map of the 'Garden of Eden' as well as more photos and additional information can be found on their web site:

www.Mauigardenofeden.com

8.) LOWER & UPPER PUOHOKAMOA FALLS
Mile Markers 10-11 - Highway 360 (★★★★☆)

Between mile markers 10-11 along the highway there are two of Mau'i's most beautiful falls, Upper & Lower Puohokamoa Falls. First we'll tell you about the lesser known of the two falls, Lower Puohokamoa Falls. Lower Puohokamoa Falls eludes nearly everyone driving the Road to Hana and here's why. As you can see via the map on the following page, you have to view the lower falls *before* the upper falls, not after like you'd think. The upper falls are right beyond mile marker 11, but the pull out for the overlook of the lower falls is about 8/10 of a mile past mile marker 10. Here there is a path leading alongside a fence that will take you to a small lookout where you'll be able to see the fall cascading 200 feet down the green cliff.

Lower Puohokamoa Falls is actually the largest waterfall you can view along the Road to Hana. The vast majority of folks get caught up at the Upper falls and miss this one entirely.

Now we'll tell you about the waterfall that's easier to reach, Upper Puohokamoa Falls. Just beyond mile marker 11 there is a bridge and beside it a small parking space (to the right) where a short path leads you to the upper falls and

picnic area, the same one you can see from the Garden of Eden. As of our last visit, the landowner (the Garden of Eden) was restricting land access to the falls, so don't be surprised if it's still closed. You can still get decent photographs from near the road.

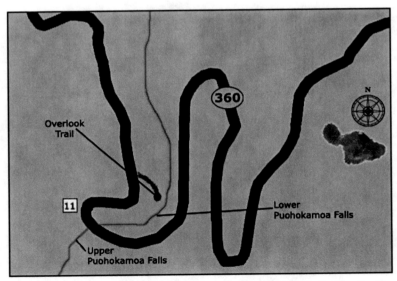

This reference map shows the Hana Highway in relation to the two waterfall locations as well as the path to the overlook.

9.) HAIPUA'ENA FALLS
Mile Marker 11 - Highway 360 (★★★☆☆)

Located 1/2 mile past mile marker 11 on the Road to Hana you'll find Haipua'ena Falls, another beautiful waterfall on the Road to Hana! There is short trail on the far side of the bridge that can give you an up close and personal view of the falls and pool. A larger fall upstream feeds Haipua'ena but the hike is usually slippery and a risk. On our last visit the lower falls was all that was easily visible. We attempted to get to the upper falls, along with some other folks, and none of us could do it (or were not willing to take the risk up the steep and muddy slope). If you're a die-hard waterfall fan, this stop might be worth the trouble to get to the falls. If not, keep on driving... there are better things ahead.

Haipua'ena Falls is a location where you can view several small picturesque waterfalls, but the best falls are still ahead of you.

10.) KAUMAHINA STATE WAYSIDE PARK
Mile Marker 12 - Highway 360 (★★★★☆)

The Keanae Peninsula can be seen from various overlooks inside Kaumahina State Wayside Park.

Just past mile marker 12 you'll find the Hana Highway's first state wayside park, Kaumahina State Wayside Park. This 7.8 acre forested rest stop offers scenic views of the northeast Mau'i coastline.

One highlight is a spectacular view of the Keanae Peninsula and village, an upcoming stop. There are also several loop trails that lead uphill from the ocean giving you a chance to view the many exotic plants. To make this spot even more attractive, in the spring/summer of 2005 it underwent a major renovation project. Expect to spend 15-30 minutes here, possibly longer if you stop for a picnic lunch or to do a bit of bird watching.

11.) HONOMANU BAY LOOKOUT
Mile Marker 13 - Highway 360 (★★☆☆☆)

Right beyond Kauma-
hina State Wayside
Park you'll find a pull-
out that gives a good
view of Honomanu
Bay. From this vantage
point you can get an-
other good look at the
Keanae Peninsula.

*This lookout of Honomanu Bay may give you the opportunity to
watch some local surfers in action. You also have another
opportunity to catch a glimpse of Keanae Peninsula (top right)
from this location.*

12.) PUNALAU VALLEY FALLS
Mile Marker 13 - Highway 360 (★★★★☆)

If you've been looking for a waterfall you can enjoy all to yourself, you might be in luck at this next spot. This previously unknown falls has become known as Punalau Falls due to the fact it is located on Punalau Stream (makes sense). Punalau Falls is a very tranquil waterfall with its waters sliding down the steep slope at the end of the small Punalau Valley.

To access the falls, pull off on the far side of the bridge around a quarter-mile past mile marker 13. If you head up the Punalau streambed while doing some serious rock skipping, at around 800 or so feet up the valley, you should reach the falls. If you're lucky, you'll have the falls all to yourself. The walk up the streambed on the rocks can take anywhere from 10-25 minutes one way. Since the short trek is relatively tricky, we'd recommend a good sense of balance for this special treat. If the stream is flowing heavily or the weather threatens rain, we'd recommend skipping this falls.

Punalau Falls can take some time to get to by slow rock skipping, but the rewarding view at the end is worth it.

ROAD TO HANA

*Parked, walked down, up second road & back
along hwy to car.*

13.) HONOMANU BAY ROAD
Mile Marker 14 - Highway 360 (★★☆☆☆)

Right after mile marker 14 you will have a chance to visit Honomanu Bay, which you just saw from above at mile marker 13. If you are looking to get to the ocean, the access road is available for you to go down to a nice black sand beach. It's a favorite hang-out for locals (somewhat similar to the Ho'okipa crowd we mentioned before).

Like many beaches in Hawai'i, the amount of sand can vary from the winter to summer months. In the winter months the beach can be mostly small rocks and boulders. Whereas, in the summer the sand will return. There are no signs or markers for this spot. There are also no facilities. In our opinion, the best way to view this bay is from above (at mile marker 13 or 14). After you enjoy its beauty and snap a few photos, you can continue on your way.

14.) ROAD TO HANA HIGHWAY LOOKOUTS
Mile Marker 14 - Highway 360 (★★★★★)

Between mile markers 14 and 16 there are several dirt and/ or broken pavement pullouts on the left side of the road that will provide really beautiful lookouts. Most are as good as any other, but the two we've noted below are our personal favorites and are worth a quick stop.

Off to the left, around mile marker 14, there is a pullout that overlooks the Hana Highway and Honomanu Bay back to your left (photo - below). This is a perfect location to take a picture of the winding highway along with Honomanu Bay. This is one of our favorite lookouts on the highway.

The overlook near mile marker 14 is perhaps the most famous and popular photo spot along the Hana Highway. The winding highway can be seen across Honomanu Bay as it winds its way along the lush coast of Mauʻi's north east shore.

The lookout near mile marker 16 is equally as impressive as the previous one, only it offers a completely different viewing angle that is absolutely stunning. Most people surprisingly miss this spot because you have to climb up the hill to see the view.

Down the road a bit further is another pullout, this time on a steep embankment with trees on top. This is the last place you can see such an expansive view of the highway as it twists and turns around the shore heading for Hana Town. What makes it our favorite, however, is that while the Road to Hana is impressive on the left, the view of Keanae Peninsula on the right is incredible from this vantage point.

15.) NUA'AILUA BAY & SCENIC LOOKOUT
Mile Marker 16 - Highway 360 (★★★★☆)

From mile marker 16 (which is missing a physical marker) you can look back and get an excellent view of steep and rugged Nua'ailua Bay to your left. This vantage point is quite different from the previous lookout – notice the cliff-like walls channeling the waves into this bay, versus the gently slopping shoreline of Honomanu. This quick change in topography can be caused by a combination of lava flow patterns and wave action over millions of years.

16.) KEANAE ARBORETUM & GARDEN
Mile Marker 16 - Highway 360 (★★★★☆)

Around 1/2 mile beyond mile marker 16 you'll see a sign on the right that says Keanae Arboretum, this is our next stop. The arboretum is pretty large with a paved parking lot off to the left after the sign. Because of the sloped curve in the road, be careful crossing the street from the parking area to the arboretum.

The Keanae Arboretum lies alongside the Pi'inaau Stream on leveled terraces built hundreds of years ago by Hawaiians for growing taro, a mainstay of their diet. A 0.6 mile paved walkway takes visitors through timber, fruit, and ornamental trees from tropical regions around the world, many of which are marked with name plates. Inside the arboretum you can find some 150 varieties of tropical plants (including taro). This is a great location to see some indigenous flowers and the famous painted bark eucalyptus trees.

An upper section of the arboretum features plants cultivated by the Hawaiians for food and other uses. This arboretum appears to have undergone a major renovation between 2002 and 2005. Our last visit included an expansion on the pre-
vious path that now leads into beautiful small taro fields not previously located in the arboretum. There is also a path through a patch of sacred Hawai'i Ti plants that provides excellent photo opportunities of what we have dubbed, "The Lone Palm" of Keanae.

Keanae Arboretum has no facilities or amenities associated with it, but it is a great location for families with children to rest along the drive to Hana. You can expect to spend anywhere from 30 minutes to an hour here.

17.) KEANAE PENINSULA & VILLAGE
Mile Marker 16 - Highway 360 (★★★★☆)

Immediately after leaving Keanae Arboretum you're in for a real treat. You'll notice a road that splits off the highway to the left with a sign labeled "Keanae Peninsula." Be sure to take a moment to visit the peninsula (the same one you saw earlier from Kaumahina Wayside Park or another lookout). From here you can get a really great view of the rugged northeast Mau'i coastline, plus you can watch the huge waves crash on the lava shores of Keanae. From this location you are exactly 18 miles from Hana.

18.) CHING'S POND (SAPPHIRE POOLS)
Mile Marker 16 - Highway 360 (★★★☆☆)

About 8/10 mile past mile marker 16, you'll notice there is a bridge over the Keanae Stream. You likely will not be able to view any of the pools or the falls from the road. Access is via two trails on the left side of the bridge before you cross it. A word of wisdom from those who have lived and learned on taking the two trails here. The trail immediately next to the bridge is very steep, very difficult, and should

be avoided unless absolutely necessary. A bit further to the left of the bridge, about 30 feet over is a large tree. There is a trail here too, and it's significantly easier to get down to Ching's pond and the pools this way.

These 'sapphire blue pools' (as they are also known) are located in a constricted gorge that flushes the water through at a very quick rate before emptying into the crystal clear blue pools. Directly beneath the bridge and makai (toward the ocean) there is a naturally formed swimming pool great for a quick dip. A small water chute (falls) empties into it delivering cool water from the upper pools above. Diving into this pool is NOT recommended at any time. Local residents also tend to stop here frequently, especially on weekends.

19.) KEANAE PENINSULA LOOKOUT
Mile Marker 17 - Highway 360 (★★★☆☆)

Around mile marker 17 there is an easy-to-miss pull off to the left side of the road. If you are able to spot it, make sure you stop. From this location you can get a really fantastic view overlooking the Keanae Peninsula (where you stopped just earlier). This is also a great location to photograph the scenic Mau'i coast. A short stop should suffice here for a few minutes to look and take pictures.

20.) WAILUA VALLEY STATE PARK
Mile Marker 18 - Highway 360 (★★☆☆☆)

About 6/10 mile past mile marker 18, on the right, you'll come to Wailua Valley State Wayside Park. This "park" is a small rest area (parking lot) that most people blow right by and never even realize it's there. It's so discrete we nearly miss it every time. The park offers an excellent viewpoint of the northern Mau'i coast and Wailua area. The park provides perspectives of the Keanae Valley, Ko'olau Gap in Haleakala's crater and Wailua Village. It's not a major attraction, but it's worth a stop for some great coastal views. After parking, take the stairs up to the lookout on your right. You can expect to spend about 10-15 minutes at this location.

The view from the parking lot doesn't reveal much, but a short hike up the stairs and you'll be rewarded with this picturesque view of Wailua town below.

21.) WAIKANI (THREE BEARS) FALLS
Mile Marker 19 - Highway 360 (★★★★★)

As we continue down the highway, our next stop is about 3/10 mile past mile marker 19. Here you'll find beautiful Three Bears Falls. This is one of the most visited waterfalls in this area. It is also locally known as the Upper Waikani Falls. At first glance it appears as though your only view will be from the roadside, but further investigation yields a short trail to the falls. At the Hana end of the bridge you will see a way to climb under the structure; some folks say to climb under on the mauka (mountain) side, but we found it easier on the makai (ocean) side. After climbing under the bridge, follow the short jungle-like path towards the falls and then rock-skip a few feet up to the best vantage point. This is a really great way to view the falls up close and personal. The falls can change in size dramatically depending on rainfall. In the winter months the falls can be huge, whereas in the spring and summer they can be much smaller (as seen above), but still a beautiful stop regardless of water flow.

MAP OF THE ROAD TO HANA
Mile Markers 19 - 34

...Continued from page 3

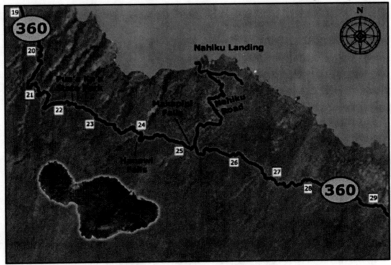

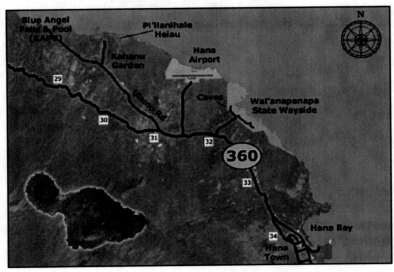

Map continues on page 46...

22.) PUAʻA KAʻA STATE WAYSIDE PARK
Mile Marker 22 - Highway 360 (★★★☆☆)

Further down the high-way, around 6/10 mile past mile marker 22, we arrive at the third state wayside park on the journey, Puaʻa Kaʻa State Wayside Park. This lovely park has a trail that provides an easy walk to several small falls.

Mongooses (yes that's plural) also hang out here. You may have already seen them streaking across the road. Some bright soul imported them to kill the rats that the sailors brought here on their boats. Well, they killed the ground rats and all the ground birds but left the tree rats.

The mongooses run around this area gathering food left over from picnics. You are also likely to see the wild Mauʻi chickens that frequent the area.

The paved parking lot at this location will be off to your left. Rest rooms and picnic spots are available as well. You can expect to spend 15-30 minutes here, perhaps longer if you stop for a picnic or do some exploring (trailblazing).

23.) LAVA TUBES & CAVES
Mile Markers 22 - Highway 360 (★☆☆☆☆)

As you continue on, you may notice the lava tubes/caves beyond mile marker 22. They are worth a short stop but they aren't anything you won't see again, like at Waiʻanapanapa State Wayside Park later in our journey. The first time we went looking for them we walked up and down the road several times before discovering they weren't anything super impressive. "Oh look, a hole with roots." Waiʻanapanapa is much better!

Lava caves are Mother Nature's way of channeling red-hot lava from the volcano's vents to the sea. Lava caves are frequently found on the younger islands in the Hawaiian chain, such as Mauʻi and the Big Island, but are rarely seen on the older islands like Kauaʻi and Oahu, as they have collapsed over time. It is awe-inspiring to peer into these long caverns imagining the lava flows that once traversed through them unknown to all those above.

24.) HANAWI FALLS
Mile Marker 24.1 - Highway 360 (★★★☆☆)

Our next official stop is right after mile marker 24. Here you'll find Hanawi Falls. This is one of many falls that the Hanawi Stream creates in its nine-mile path to the ocean. Because the stream is spring-fed, many of the falls can even be seen during the drier summer months. A large rain shower can have a great effect on the flow of the Hanawi Falls. The safest way to view the falls is from the bridge. Attempting to hike up or down the stream in order to see other waterfalls is very slippery, not to mention dangerous. This is probably why you'll notice private property signs up around the location. Across the road is a small building that serves some purpose we haven't quite determined yet; we suspect something to do with irrigation. It also should be treated as private property.

25.) MAKAPIPI FALLS
Mile Marker 25 - Highway 360 (★★★★☆)

As you take the bridge over Makapipi stream near mile marker 25 be sure to stop to check out the falls under the bridge. Here you'll find Makapipi Falls, one of the most interesting falls on the Hana Highway. The Makapipi Stream flows within the lava streambed into a pristine blue pool. The Hana Highway crosses directly over the stream allowing for a beautiful view of the falls over the bridge railing. The flow of the falls is dependent on rainfall, but if caught at the right time it can offer a spectacular experience.

To access this location, park just beyond the bridge where there is a small pull off and walk back onto the bridge to look down.

Makapipi Falls is a spectacle most people will never see, a waterfall directly from above cascading into the pool below.

26.) NAHIKU ROAD & LANDING
Mile Marker 25 - Highway 360 (★★★★★)

Just a few yards past mile marker 25 you should see a steep downhill turn off for Nahiku Road on your left. If you go down this road (about 2.5 miles) you'll come to the gorgeous scenic bay. It is easy to miss this spot, but it's an awesome place to stop and has some great scenery. The coastal views are some of the very best on the entire road to Hana. The vegetation along this road and in the area is absolutely amazing and makes for some great photo opportunities.

Another thing fascinating to us about this spot is the sound created by the thousands of pebbles being rubbed against

the shore. It's a very unique sound. You can best experience this harmonic treat off to the right of where you park, down on the shore. You can expect to spend about 15-45 minutes here.

From this point forward much of the "enclosed" feel of the highway starts to open up a bit as you get closer and closer to Hana Town. You'll also start to pass more houses and developed areas. Here's a quick synopsis of what you'll see between Nahiku Landing and our next stop at Ula'ino Road. Just beyond mile marker 26 you'll pass some houses, some garden and floral stands, and eventually you'll pass by some run-down looking areas right beyond mile marker 27. The heavy rain makes everything look 10-15 years older than it really is here. You'll also start to get some pretty good views of Haleakala's north east face. Closer to mile marker 30 you'll really notice the road opening up to fantastic scenery of the Pacific Ocean north of Mau'i. At mile marker 31 you'll officially be welcomed to Hana Town with a sign, and shortly thereafter you'll see the turn off for the small Hana airport. Next stop... Ula'ino Road.

Nahiku Landing offers some of the very best coastal views along the Road to Hana. It is a great place to have a picnic or a snack as you continue on your journey to Hana Town.

27.) PI'ILANI HEIAU & KAHANU GARDEN
Mile Marker 31 - On Ula'ino Road - (★★★☆☆)

Our next stop, located on Ula'ino Road off the Hana Highway, is about half a mile beyond mile marker 31. Here you'll find the Kahanu Garden, and inside is Hawai'i's oldest and largest place of worship available to visitors today, Pi'ilanihale Heiau. It was constructed completely out of lava rock in the 14th century at the same time the Pi'ilani Dynasty ruled.

The Kahanu Garden, which is known for its extensive collection of breadfruit trees, is an extension of the National Tropical Botanical Garden.

As of this printing, the garden is open Monday - Friday, 10am - 2pm. Admission costs: Adults - $10; Children – Free. It closes without notice, so don't be surprised if you find "Closed" signs.

Despite the admission price, visiting a heiau is a very unique and culturally educating experience you don't want to miss. Be sure to check this spot out but be careful when driving down Ula'ino Road, it can be muddy and hard to navigate at times. If it has recently rained, you may want to avoid driving on the road completely.

28.) BLUE ANGEL FALLS & BLUE POOL (KAPU)
Mile Marker 31 - On Ula'ino Road (☆☆☆☆☆☆)

OK, first things first. This spot was given a lot of attention by a popular guidebook. And by a lot of attention, we do mean *a lot*. A few thousand visitors a day now head down muddy Ula'ino Road to view the falls, and to do so, they must ALL cross private property. This has caused quite a few problems in the area. As you approach the end of Ula'ino Road, you'll notice several lots and people now charging for parking (it used to all be free). Then, after you park and head down the road to the ocean you'll be bombarded with "NO TRESPASSING" signs left and right, meaning it is kapu (off limits). The beach is public access, but getting to it is not. So, with that in mind, you can decide if this spot is for you. In our opinion, the waterfall isn't that great and isn't worth the risk of being charged with trespassing by angry landowners. And who can blame them? If you had a thousand people a day tromping through your backyard, it'd probably upset you too. This may be a good chance to show some Aloha and just skip this spot.

Definitely work a couple of hours. good beach spot.

ROAD TO HANA

29.) WAI'ANAPANAPA STATE WAYSIDE PARK
Mile Marker 32 - Highway 360 (★★★★☆)

Getting closer to the end of our journey we have one last major stop at mile marker 32. On the left side of the highway you should see a gravel road leading down to the park. There should also be a road sign informing you of this location. Here you will find Wai'anapanapa State Wayside Park.

Wai'anapanapa   (Why-Ah-naa-paa-naa-paa)   features sculpted lava rocks, wind twisted foliage, a sea arch, lava caves and tubes, and even a black sand beach named Pa'iloa. There's even a 'blow hole' in the lava rocks near the shoreline. The snorkeling and diving can be great here, but unfortunately, it is seldom very calm. Visibility is almost always low. Swimming is possible, but caution should be exercised. The beach is open to the ocean with no outside reef to break the force of the waves and current. The water can be very rough at this location. You will see many warning signs in place because of this. Beach access is located to the left of the main parking area.

The black sand beach isn't the only attraction at Wai'anapanapa though. Pa'iloa is a beach with 'wild' surroundings. The area around the park is very interesting to hike through. There are a few "wet" caves and lava tubes with pure, fresh water running through them. They can be reached by walking beyond the beach access denoted above or you can just look for trail signs. There are also a few lava tubes extending from the shoreline into the water.

This is a visually stunning area with many historical points of interest. There are a large variety of sea birds here for the bird watching enthusiasts as well. Rest rooms and picnic tables are available. Expect to spend about half an hour or more depending on how much exploring you do.

30.) HANA TOWN, BAY, & RANCH
Mile Markers 33 to 34 - End of Hwy 360 (★★★★☆)

After leaving Wai'anapanapa State Park you'll turn left back onto the highway and pass the Hana Town schools just before entering Hana Town itself. You will come to a fork in the road at the entrance of the town, the left fork takes you down to Hana Bay in about a mile, and the right fork takes you into "downtown" Hana with its stores, shops, and restaurants. The right fork is also the direct route to Highway 31 and all the adventures that lie beyond Hana Town.

But now that you're at the end of your journey, let's take a moment to explore more about Hana Town. Hana is a 4,500 acre area previously owned by the Unna Brothers who, in the 1800's, raised sugar cane. In 1935, the area was bought by Paul Fagan who began raising cattle in the area. Today the Hana area is owned by Keola Hana Mau'i, Inc. which also continues to raise cattle on 2,200 acres.

Today Hana is a quaint little town that offers Mau'i visitors a place to relax away from the mainstream lives they've almost all come to escape. Hana is certainly the place to go to get away from it all. In Hana you can grab a bite to eat at one of the many small restaurants or shops, you can go shopping in one of the many small stores, and you can even talk story (chat) with some of the local folks. We always like to joke with them about the cars parked on the Hana Highway and the fact that they have been there for about two decades now. "Oh they're part of the scenery of the highway now, just too expensive to tow them out," they say with a smile. And in Hana town, a smile is about as genuine a smile as you'll ever find. While you're in Hana make sure to also take a moment and visit Hana Bay and the local red sand (Kaihalulu) beach.

This sign welcomes you to Hana a good while before you actually enter the town itself. We find it amusing how every town sign on Mau'i says it is "THE" historic town on the island. Fortunately, Hana really is one of the best towns on all of Mau'i.

BEYOND HANA
& UP COUNTRY MAUI

You haven't experienced a sunset in Hawai'i until you've seen one from the upcountry of Mau'i.

The Pipiwai Trail at the Ohe'o Gulch (page 61) is perhaps the most rewarding trail on the entire island of Mau'i. With two giant waterfalls, several smaller ones, a number of swimming pools, and a bamboo forest that's out of this world you are sure to be delighted with this hiking adventure.

Pipiwai trail is just one of the many amazing adventures that await you on the Beyond Hana drive into the Upcountry.

BEYOND HANA TOWN
Highway 31 to Highway 37

So you've driven the Road to Hana and you want more? Maybe you'd like to see some gorgeous waterfalls or one of the world's most beautiful beaches? If so... continuing beyond Hana Town on Highway 31 is for you. Highway 31 will take you to Alau Island, world famous Hamoa Beach, Wailua Falls, the Oheʻo Gulch (7 Pools), South Haleakala, and much more as it continues around the island into the upcountry of Mauʻi where it turns into newly paved Highway 37.

After driving the Road to Hana many people will discover they just don't have the time to make the drive beyond Hana in the same day. Thus, there is a long-standing debate about whether it's smarter to stop in Hana for the night, or to try and get up really early and make the non-stop drive to Hana, only then start on the other side. Our recommendation — stay in Hana. It's not the cheapest place to stay the night, but unless you're looking to get up at 5 am in paradise and drive 3 hours to Hana, just to begin your sight-seeing, you're going to want to spend the night in Hana Town. Even if you got started at 8 am you'd be far ahead of the crowd. That said, the choice will be yours to make, but we highly recommend you stop for the night in Hana Town, and thus start your morning in Hana. That's where we'll begin, entering town.

MAP OF THE ROAD BEYOND HANA
Mile Markers 51 - 38

...Continued from page 31

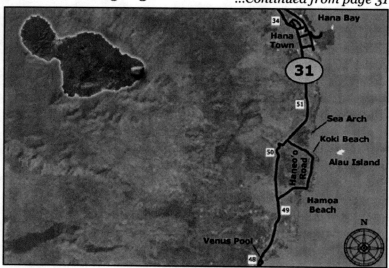

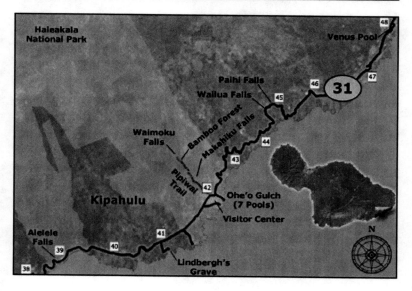

1.) STARTING POINT - HANA TOWN
Junction of Highway 360 & Highway 31 (★★★★☆)

If you haven't explored Hana Town, and you have some spare time, then we definitely suggest you stop for a bit and explore this remarkable small town. Life here is unique to perhaps no other place in the world. It is a slow pace for some, but it's as real as it gets. The food is as fresh as you'll find, the people friendlier than anywhere we've certainly ever been, and the atmosphere is relaxed and calm. All your worries are free to slip away here. Yes, it is fair to say that in Hana a person can find pono (good) in nearly all they experience. With that said, if you didn't explore Hana, flip back to page 42 for more details on Hana and what you can do there.

Hana Bay is a great place to stretch your legs after a long day's ride. The large black sand beach invites you to take a swim, and it's one of the safest spots to swim on east Mauʻi. Also, if you go exploring, please be sure to respect "No Trespassing" signs.

Once you've seen beautiful Hana, you'll likely be eager to begin your journey beyond. At the far edge of Hana Town after taking the right fork you'll almost unknowingly leave Highway 360 (Hana Highway) and begin on Highway 31 (S. Hana Highway), heading towards Highway 37. It is important to note that the mile markers leading away from Hana Town are COUNTING DOWN, not up. This is opposite what you experienced coming into Hana Town. On Highway 31 you should also be aware that the mile markers count down until mile marker 15, then they jump back to 20 and go down again. Don't say we didn't warn you about mile markers being a little weird on Mau'i.

This 'Baby Pigs Crossing' sign has become famous on the internet. We're not exactly sure what all the fuss is about, but several folks have taken delight in it. So if you're looking to see it for yourself, it'll be up on a tree on the right side of the road as you leave Hana Town.

2.) HANEO'O ROAD & ANCIENT FISHPONDS
Mile Marker 51 - On Haneo'o Road (★★★★☆)

Right beyond Hana Town heading down Highway 31 you'll come to a road on the left named Haneo'o Road, right around mile marker 51. Haneo'o Road heads down towards the coast to several ancient Hawaiian fishponds, Alau Island, Koki Beach, Hamoa Beach, and a small community of homes. The road practically parallels Highway 31 for several miles before rejoining the highway approximately two miles from where you left it. If it has just rained, you may find the first portion of this road a little muddy, but rest assured the conditions improve further down this road.

The map below shows more detail on Haneo'o Road and the sights to visit along it. Our next two stops are also on Haneo'o Road.

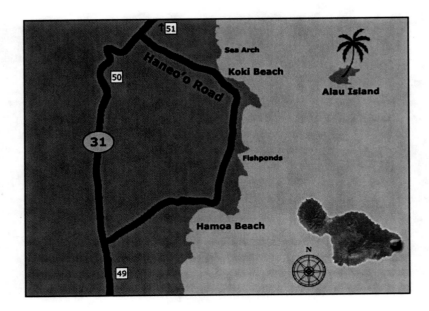

50

3.) KOKI BEACH & ALAU ISLAND
Haneoʻo Road - Off Highway 31 (★★★☆☆)

As you drive down Haneoʻo Road, the rugged cliffs give way to a beautiful coastal view. As you continue down towards the shore you'll notice Alau Island off in the distance. Look to your left and you'll also be able to view a sea arch off in the distant on the rocky coast, a really beautiful backdrop to the scene.

There are only a few sea arches on Mauʻi that are both easy to get to and look great in photographs (due to their pristine surround-ings) - this is one of them. Plus you have beautiful Koki Beach and Alau Island offshore to make the view even better.

If you didn't know what was ahead you'd probably think Koki Beach, with Alau Island offshore, was one of the most remarkable beaches you'd ever seen. Unfortunately, down a road a bit it has some serious competition - world famous Hamoa Beach.

About 100 yards down the road as it starts to level off, you'll notice a pull off to the left. This is the Koki Beach overlook. From here you can also get an excellent view of the Alau Island with its swaying palms directly offshore. You can get onto the beach by taking one of the trails leading down to it, but we highly recommend you do not swim at this beach because of strong currents and surf. Don't fret. A better swimming beach is just ahead. Also, be careful on the left side of the parking area, as the cliff overlooking the beach from this area can be quite high. A little bit further down the road you will come to our next stop, beautiful Hamoa Beach.

4.) HAMOA BEACH
Haneoʻo Road - Off Highway 31 (★★★★★)

Heading a bit further
down the road beyond
Koki Beach and Alau
Island you'll discover
one of the most beau-
tiful beaches in all of
Hawaiʻi -- world fa-
mous Hamoa Beach.

After parking in the lot
at the beach, proceed down the stairs to the shoreline. The
grounds around the beach are nearly as captivating as the
beach itself. Hamoa Beach is about 1,000 feet long and about
100 feet wide with sea cliffs surrounding it. Surrounded by
all the vegetation, it is absolutely stunning.

Off shore there is decent snorkeling and scuba diving, good
swimming, and just as in ancient times, excellent surfing
too (but only when the waves are up, mostly in the winter).
If you can wrestle a kayak down to the beach, launching is
relatively easy when the surf is down. Hamoa is unprotected
by fringing reefs, so big surf hits the beach unimpeded in the
winter months.

The beach is surrounded by private property owned by the
Hotel Hana Mauʻi. Most of the facilities are for the guests of
the resort, but the resort is gracious enough to allow the use
of some of the facilities. There are rest rooms, showers, and
picnic tables available for you to use here. You can expect to
spend about half an hour or more depending on swimming
times, etc.

After leaving the beach you'll continue on down Haneo'o Road, passing several small communities and houses. There really isn't much to see beyond Hamoa Beach, so we recommend you just drive straight back to the highway. When you do reach Highway 31 again you'll want to turn left to continue your journey. You will be getting on right before mile marker 49 (remember, the mile markers are now counting down). From here you'll continue on Highway 31 towards some of the best and most beautiful spots on Mau'i.

The lush tropical setting at Hamoa Beach makes it one of the most beautiful beaches on the entire island. As you park and head down the stairs to the beach below, take a moment to observe all the beautiful flowers and plants around the beach. If you're lucky and visit during the spring/summer, you'll likely get the chance to see some plumeria trees up close along the edge of the road.

5.) VENUS POOL
Mile Marker 48 - Highway 31 (★★★★☆)

Venus Pool, also known locally as Waikoa Pond, is a beautiful and remote swimming pool next to the ocean. This naturally formed pool was once used exclusively by the ali'i (royalty) of Hawai'i. As you drive down Highway 31, it'll be near mile marker 48, between Hana and the Ohe'o Gulch Pools. Venus Pool isn't the well kept secret it once was, but if you're lucky, you still might have the pool all to yourself. The freshwater swimming pool has become quite popular with folks looking to avoid the crowds further down at the Ohe'o Gulch. Swimming is great here and the water is very calm, but the end of the pool where the stream enters the ocean should be avoided due to undertow.

To access the pool you'll want to park at mile marker 48 on Hana Highway before the bridge. There is no marker

for the trail and at first glance there appears to be nothing here. That's likely why so many folks rush on by towards the Ohe'o Gulch and 7 Pools. Once you've parked, you'll likely notice that on the other

side of the barbed wire
fence there is a well-worn
footpath through the field
that parallels the stream.

When you reach what
appears to be a large hollow
rock (an old bread oven)
in the middle of the field
next to the path, turn right toward the stream and take the
path down to the smooth rocks above the stream. If for any
reason you don't feel comfortable jumping or going through
the fence (we didn't at first), you can also walk towards the
ocean along the streambed by going under the bridge on
the ocean side of the road. This route is MUCH harder than
walking through the field, but you won't technically be on
private property this way.

The mauka (inland) view from Venus Pool is also very captivating.

6.) WAILUA FALLS
Mile Marker 45 - Highway 31 (★★★★★)

Seven miles south of Hana at mile marker 45 off Highway 31 you'll reach one of the most gorgeous falls in all of Hawai'i, Wailua Falls. You will cross a bridge where its stream waters cross under the road. If you're coming from Hana Town, it'll be on your right. There is a parking lot immediately off to the left after you pass the falls.

Wailua Falls gracefully cascades 200 feet through a lush setting in the surrounding vegetation just feet from the road. There is a short path to the base of the falls, and some people even like to swim

there. Watch your step when taking the path to the falls as it can be very slippery. The early morning sun really showcases the drama that Wailua Falls has to offer.

The water flow of Wailua Falls varies but is usually pretty at any rate and any time of the year. Even during drier times, the falls is still usually showering water down onto the rocks below. However, this waterfall is photogenic regardless of flow rate. Expect this to be about a 20-minute visit.

Pua'a Lu'u Falls and another small waterfall are both located a little farther down the road from Wailua Falls. There's a pullout on the side of the road past the bridge at Pua'a Lu'u Falls, and the short path downstream to the falls is also worth a brief stop.

The recent weather can have a significant impact on the flow rate of Wailua Falls. Just compare the photograph above (during a dry spell) to the photograph on the previous page (a day after it rained) and you can clearly see the difference. Regardless of flow rate, the falls is one of the most beautiful on Mau'i.

7.) OHE'O GULCH (SEVEN SACRED POOLS)
Mile Marker 44 - Highway 31 (★★★★★)

About 15 minutes past Hana, near mile marker 44, is the Ohe'o Gulch at the east end of Haleakala National Park. The Ohe'o Gulch is known by many names. Some call it the Kipahulu Area, while others call it the location of the Seven Sacred Pools.

Whatever you decide to call the spot, this series of waterfalls emptying into natural pools which flow through the Ohe'o Gulch into the ocean nearby is one of the best spots to visit on Mau'i. You're in for a real treat here. There are numerous pools and waterfalls, great hikes (which we'll talk about shortly), a historical site and heiau nearby, picturesque settings, a ranger station, and rest rooms. After crossing the bridge over Pipiwai

Stream, the parking lot is located on the left side of the road. The fee for visiting the park is only $10 per vehicle and is valid for this part of Haleakala National Park, as well as the road that leads to the summit of Haleakala (page 81).

The Pipiwai Stream is the source of water for all of the falls in this area, which number far greater than just seven. In fact, the

The Pipiwai stream is like most others on East Maui in that it can be greatly affected by the weather. Compare the photo above, after a day of rain to the one on the previous page which was taken during a moderate drought - it was May both times.

pools start some two miles inland. But the easiest to reach and the nicest pools are located near the shoreline right beyond the National Park Ranger's building. In 1969, the land where the 'Seven Sacred Pools' are situated (formally known as 'Kipahulu coastal area') was donated to the Haleakala National Park system so that the pools would forever be open to the public. Today both visitors from afar and locals alike enjoy swimming in these magnificently pristine pools.

On the next few pages we'll cover all the exciting things to do in this area, especially regarding hiking, as many of these places are only accessible by trail. They are some of the most gorgeous hidden gems on Maui, so don't miss them.

Kipahulu Area (Oheʻo Gulch) Hiking Guide

There are a variety of hikes in this area. Many are known as the Kipahulu Area Trails. All of the following trails start at the Visitor Center:

Kuloa Point Trail

A .5 mile (.8km) easy loop trail leads from the Kipahulu Visitor Center down to the ocean at Kuloa Point past historic walls and pre-contact Hawaiian habitation sites. The trail passes a grove of hala trees on the way to beautiful views of the ocean and several large pools. Swimming is at your own risk. There are no lifeguards on duty. Serious injuries and deaths have occurred due to people jumping into the water from the cliffs above. The ocean currents at Kuloa Point are very strong and sharks and high surf are constant dangers. Do not go into the ocean here.

Kahakai Trail

The Kahakai Trail stretches .25 mile (.54km) between Kuloa Point and the Kipahulu campground. Shoreline views along the ocean are beautiful... but watch your step along cliff sides!

Pipiwai Trail

The most famous of all the trails in this area is the Pipiwai Trail (our next stop). Located above the Seven Sacred Pools, it is one of the best hikes on Mauʻi. It is 4 miles roundtrip, gaining 650-feet in elevation. It takes 2 1/2 - 5 hours to hike, depending on how long you linger. There are several waterfalls along the way, but the grand prize is the massive Waimoku Falls, which drops 400-feet down a lava rock wall. This was absolutely beautiful and more than well worth the hike to get to it.

Trail Information Source: National Park Service

8.) PIPIWAI TRAIL
Mile Marker 44 at the Oheʻo Gulch (★★★★★)

The Pipiwai Trail is a moderately strenuous 4-mile round-trip trail. The trailhead is right past the bridge that passes over Pipiwai stream on the mauka (mountain) side of the highway. The trail winds up hill along the  edge of Pipiwai Stream past several waterfalls and pools. The remains of a sugar mill dam, irrigation systems, and flumes of the late 1800s can be seen in several places along the trail. The first 0.5 mile heads up gently sloping meadows to an overlook of the beautiful 184-foot Makahiku Falls (see next page). You will also encounter a giant banyan tree along the way (photograph on page 127). In another half mile you enter a woodland of mixed ohiʻa and koa. Continue your hike over foot-bridges above the stream and through lush tropical forests of introduced bamboo, mango and guava to where the trail ends near the base of the 400-foot Waimoku Falls (see next page).

Be prepared for rain, mud, and slippery mosses. Mosquitoes are very friendly here at times, especially in the wetter winter months. Be sure to bring bottled water if you hike. There are several waterfall pools to swim in along the way, so bring a bathing suit and towel. You can expect to spend a total of about 2-3 hours at this location, including stops.

9.) MAKAHIKU & WAIMOKU FALLS
On Pipiwai Trail - Highway 31 (★★★★★)

Makahiku Falls is along the Pipiwai Trail, above Seven Sacred Pools as it heads towards Waimoku Falls. Makahiku Falls cascades a phenomenal 184-feet. The trail to the falls follows the Pipiwai Stream and at about 800 paces (0.5 mile) into the hike you'll come to the falls. When flowing, it is a sight to behold. Unfortunately, it has a tendency to dry up in the summer when there is less rain. However, we've seen it

Makahiku Falls

in the summer several different ways... heavily flowing one time and dry as a bone another. There is a small sign noting the location of the falls along the trail. Ask the park rangers about the falls if you want to know about their current flow rates before hiking.

After the falls we highly recommend you continue up the path towards the majestic Waimoku Falls. Regardless of the weather, Waimoku is almost always flowing strong. At about one mile further up the trail beyond Makahiku Falls you will enter the first of three bamboo forests. Because of the marshy ground, wooden boardwalks have been built to make hiking easier. Once you arrive at the bamboo forest, you'll definitely feel like you've stepped into another world. Despite not being native to Hawai'i, the bamboo is really quite beautiful. Over 30 feet tall, this exotic forest is cool and dark and even quite spooky. The winds that funnel up from the sea cause the leafy tops of the bamboo to sway, and as the poles below knock together in the gloom, they produce sounds that are both beautiful and eerie, like primitive music. The different thicknesses of the bamboo produce tones of differing pitch, staccato-like. When the bamboo trunks scrape and rub against each other, the screeching and whistling sounds mimic creatures heard in old 1950's jungle movies. As you leave the bamboo forest, a glimpse of 400-foot Waimoku Falls can be seen ahead taking its long plunge down the face of a horseshoe-shaped cliff into a shallow pool at its base. From here you'll have to cross the streams (their depth and flow rate depend on recent rainfall) to reach the falls. You'll definitely want to cross the streams to get an up close view of Waimoku Falls, just use extreme caution.

The Waimoku Falls hike is a four-mile round trip, two hours up and an hour and a half down. Bring water, sturdy shoes (or hiking boots), a hiking pole (if you have one), insect repellent, and do NOT drink any stream water!

Waimoku Falls

64

10.) CHARLES LINDBERGH'S GRAVE
Mile Marker 41 - Highway 31 (★★☆☆☆)

Our next stop on Highway 31 is the Palapala Ho'omau Church, located 8 miles south of Hana and one mile south of the Ohe'o Gulch on the ocean side of the highway. A narrow road around mile marker 41 leads to the church. A small sign pointing left which says "Limited Parking" is tacked on the side of a tree marking the road. Surprisingly, many people miss this. Don't be one of them.

The famous aviator, Charles Lindbergh, lies at rest on the tranquil grounds of the Palapala Ho'omau Church. Charles died on August 26, 1974 after living his last days on the bountiful Hana coast. Shortly before he died he sketched out a simple design for his grave and coffin. The church was built in 1857 and is actually made out of limestone coral. Lindbergh's grave is located behind the church under the shade of a Java plum tree. We feel the most beautiful part of this spot is the surrounding scenery. The coastal views down beyond the grave site and gardens are very exquisite.

The coastal scenery down beyond Charles Lindbergh's grave site is absolutely beautiful. Hope you brought enough film!

11.) THE ROUGH & BUMPY ROAD
Beyond Mile Marker 40 - Highway 31

Beyond Lindbergh's grave, the paved road will continue through more rural Mau'i. Soon you'll notice the road conditions start to quickly deteriorate. This is because the county of Mau'i does not perform regular  maintenance on the roads, and naturally they have become a bit 'rough' with age.

Here's what you can expect ahead. From mile marker 40 until 38 the road is about as narrow as it'll get for the entire drive ahead – don't fret though, it's not that bad, just drive it slowly and watch out for any blind curves. From mile marker 38 until 33 the road becomes broken pavement and/or gravel, but again, it's not that bad, just keep it slow. While many rental companies say you shouldn't drive this stretch of road (because they don't want to service anyone stuck on it), visitors drive it without incident frequently. The drive down this kapu (restricted) stretch of road, as your car rental company will call it, is spectacular enough to make you think you've left the island for another part of the world. Don't let anyone talk you out of making this drive; it is an experience you don't want to leave Mau'i without. Breathe a sigh of relief because from mile marker 33 forward, it is all paved again until the end. You can't help but laugh at the road change when you reach it too. We find it humorous every time.

So you're probably wondering what makes this part of the drive so special. Well, what's so absolutely amazing about this part of Mau'i is how different it is from the Hana Highway, the road directly across from it on the island. Haleakala stands in between these two halves of the island and the change is nothing short of amazing, a tropical rainforest on one side and prairie grassland and near desert on the other. It is beautiful though, and you can get some amazing coastal views and a rare look at the back of Haleakala's missing mountain-side that was eroded away in the distant past only to be partially filled again in the more recent (geologically speaking) flows.

The drive beyond is not the easiest road to drive on the island, but it's definitely one to provide some "Wow" on your vacation. There are many stretches that are so drastically different from the Road to Hana, just on the other side of the island, you would swear you had left Mau'i for another part of the world. From lava crops to amazing views of south Haleakala, this drive has it all.

12.) ALELELE TRAIL & FALLS
Mile Marker 39.3 - Highway 31 (★★★☆☆)

About 1/3 of a mile past Mile Marker 39 there is going to be a white bridge with Alelele written on the side of it. Here you will notice several trails moving inland towards Alelele Falls. Technically, it is also inside of Haleakala National Park, but most people spend their time at the overcrowded Ohe'o Gulch area and never visit this part of the park. Alelele Stream is easy to find, and it is about a 10-minute walk along the trail to get to this falls. There is a pullout on the left side of the road that leads to a landing where you can park the car. You may have to rock skip a bit and/or cross the stream, but keep heading towards the valley wall where the waterfall is. You won't regret it.

This waterfall is very beautiful, and hardly anybody knows it is here. As is typical with many falls on Mau'i, in the summertime this fall may not be flowing. If the weather has been especially dry, you can probably assume as much for the falls and just may want to skip this spot.

13.) MOKULAU & KAUPO STORE
Mile Marker 35 - Highway 31 (★☆☆☆☆☆)

As you travel south along Highway 31, the turnoff to Mokulau is just before mile marker 35 (on the left) and before the town of Kaupo. Turn left onto the dirt road leading toward the ocean. You will pass a church and cemetery. Park along the road and then walk to the shoreline. From here you can get some of the best views of the south east Mau'i coastline. There are also several lava outcroppings in this area.

The Kaupo Store right beyond this stop (past the 35 mile marker) is your last place to pick up snacks before reaching Tedeschi Winery near Highway 37. In our opinion, neither of these spots is worth too much of your time, and the store has been closed most every time we've passed it. You'll have better chances for coastal views and scenery ahead.

14.) KAUPO GAP LOOKOUT
Mile Marker 32.4 - Highway 31 (★★★★☆)

If any single thing makes the south east drive worthwhile, then this is it. The views of Haleakala will almost certainly amaze you. The sheer size of the volcano alone is an impressive sight.

Right beyond mile marker 32 is one of the best spots to see the Kaupo Gap, the large valley in the side of Haleakala. Would you believe that is an erosional valley? This is mother nature at work, not geologic forces like those found at Mount St. Helens (a pressurized eruption in 1980).

One thing you certainly won't miss is the wind in this location. When the trades are blowing at a nice pace, it can be some of the strongest wind felt on Mau'i. Definitely make sure you get out of the car here and look around, the scenery is awe-inspiring, even just a few steps off the road towards the ocean.

15.) POKOWAI SEA ARCH
Mile Marker 29 - Highway 31 (★★★☆☆)

As you continue on Highway 31, beyond mile marker 29, you'll discover Pokowai Sea Arch. The sea arch can be seen from the road, but the pullouts located near the shoreline are the safest spots to see and photograph this site. The Pokowai Sea Arch was formed when flowing lava from a volcano collided with the cold Pacific waters, creating an arch formation.

When observing the sea arch from this location, take a moment to notice the shore line as well. You won't find any sand beaches here, just rough, jagged, and pounded lava rock. This part of Mau'i is substantially younger than the rest of the island. Hence, you won't find any of those long white sand beaches gracing the shores - at least not for another million years or so. Consider this part of Mau'i a 'work in progress.'

16.) HIGHWAY 31 GULCH
Mile Marker 28 - Highway 31 (★★★★☆)

Around mile marker 28 on Highway 31 you'll come to a two-lane bridge (on a one lane road... go figure?), which crosses over a giant gulch. Slightly up the road before crossing the bridge is a good place to stop and photograph the gulch.

To appreciate its massive size, let a few vehicles pass by you and drive over the bridge in front of it.

As you continue on, you'll likely notice there's not much located in this part of Mau'i, but if you look around between mile markers 24 and 20 you'll see some ancient Hawaiian ruins. Hawaiians once heavily populated this area, but today it is desolate and dry. However, native Hawaiians are attempting to rebuild the area, now known as Kahikinui.

From this point onward you are entering the upcountry portion of Mau'i and are getting closer to Highway 37. But take our word for it, between here and our next major stop (Sun Yat-Sen Park), there is absolutely nothing to see, do, or witness. Enjoy the scenic highway driving ahead. Part of it even looks like a small roller coaster track for cars, and it is always fun just to drive up and down the large dips. It is also worth noting that ahead of you mile markers 19-15 are only visible coming from the other direction. Who knows why?

17.) TEDESCHI WINERY & RANCH STORE
Mile Marker 15 - Highway 31/37 (★★★☆☆)

Located off Highway 31/37 on the mauka (mountain) side of the road you'll find the Tedeschi Winery and the Ranch Store. It is before ranch headquarters and the Ulupalakua Ranch Store. This is the only commercial winery on the island of Maui.

At the winery you can sample their various award-winning wines while enjoying a free tour. A famous pineapple wine, called Maui Blanc, is a popular vintage from Tedeschi Winery. Many folks also like to enjoy samples of Maui Brut Champagne. Their tasting room, located inside a cottage originally built for Hawaii's King Kalakaua in 1874, is open daily from 9am-5pm.

If the winery isn't enough of a reason to stop, the view is. At over two thousand feet above sea level this is a splendid example of what Upcountry Maui has to offer. From this vantage point there are extensive views of both the Central Valley and West Maui Mountains.

After Tedeschi Winery, don't forget the mile markers are going to jump back to 20 again. By now you're probably like us and just don't even want to ask "Why?" anymore, but they do. And so onwards we continue up Highway 37 towards Kula.

18.) SUN YAT-SEN MEMORIAL PARK
Mile Marker 18.5 - Highway 37 (★★★☆☆)

Sun Yat-Sen is a small roadside park at mile marker 18.5 near the east end of the Kula Highway (part of state route 37), about 2400 feet above the south Mau'i coast.

From this location you can get some spectacular scenic views, including an excellent view of the surrounding Hawaiian Islands offshore: Kaho'olawe (the larger one to the left), uninhabited after decades of use as a bombing range and Molokini (the smaller one in front of Kaho'olawe), a semi-circular island. Its deep cove is a very popular snorkeling spot. Off to your left, near the shoreline, is the Pu'u Ola'i cinder cone in Makena State Park. Directly ahead of you on the horizon is Lana'i and to your right are the West Mau'i Mountains, likely draped in clouds.

One last great thing about this vantage point is the incredible sunsets. If you are lucky enough to be at this location late in the day before the sun sets, you will get a color show unlike anything you've ever seen. As the sun sinks over the island of Lana'i in front of you it makes for a sunset you'll remember forever (page 44).

Beyond this park the area begins to become more developed. You may find several small pull-outs that interest you, or you can just continue on your way.

19.) HIGHWAY 37 & 377 (JUNCTION 1)
Mile Marker 14 - Onto Lower Haleakala Highway 37

As you ease your way back into civilization, around mile marker 14, you'll come to the first of two junctions of Highways 37 and 377. At the first junction, stay on Highway 37, we're going to take you to the stops along that route first. When you reach the second junction, take a right onto Highway 377 and then we'll take a look at those stops. The map below, along with the corresponding arrows, should help clarify this drive.

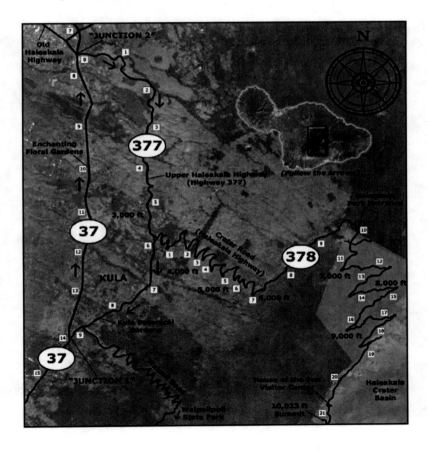

20.) ENCHANTING FLORAL GARDENS
Mile Marker 10 – Highway 37 (★★★☆☆)

Near mile marker 10 on Highway 37 you'll find a sign on the right side informing you of our next stop, the Enchanting Floral Gardens. The Enchanting Floral Gardens in Kula, Mau'i, has eight acres of walking tours displaying over 1,500 species of tropical and semi-tropical plants and flowers from around the world. The more you stroll up the path the more rewarding it is. The garden has a wide variety of exotic flowers such as proteas, orchids, hibiscus, jade vines and a variety of fruit trees. Some have complained the gardens are not maintained well, but overall we were pleased with it and found the price of $5 (per adult) reasonable. It's not the nicest garden on the island, but it's still worth a stop.

The vining Passion flower is a beautiful addition to Hawai'i.

21.) HIGHWAY 37 & 377 (JUNCTION 2)
Mile Marker 8 - Onto Upper Haleakala Highway 377

Our next "stop" isn't really a stop; it's just a junction to note. The junction of Highways 37 and 377 (this would be the second junction if coming from the road beyond Hana, the first if coming from Kahului/Pa'ia) is the beginning of the Upper Haleakala Highway.

As you travel along Highway 37 and 377, the lower and upper Haleakala Highways respectively, make sure to keep your eyes open for pull-outs on the side of the road offering some absolutely outstanding views of coastal south east Maui. From various locations you can get fantastic views of West Maui, Lana'i, Kaho'olawe, and Molokini. In general, this is also an excellent area to watch some gorgeous sunsets. Sun Yat-Sen park (page 74) is one of our favorite "sunset spots."

22.) HIGHWAY 378 (CRATER ROAD) TURN OFF
Mile Marker 6 – Highway 377

Highway 377 is only nine miles long before rejoining with Highway 37, but the first six miles are officially the Upper Haleakala Highway. Right before mile marker six, you'll find the turn off (on the left) to Highway 378, which is known as Crater Road (also the Haleakala Highway). Highway 378 will take you to the summit of Mount Haleakala and to the remainder of Haleakala National Park. This is a whole day's journey in itself, and you likely won't have time to visit it all with anything less than several (6+) hours to spare. You can learn more about the Haleakala Highway drive in the next part of this book, starting on page 81.

Highway 378 (starting page 81) is from top to bottom one of the most diverse drives in the world. Starting at near 3,500 feet and topping off on Haleakala's summit at 10,023 feet - change is all around as you pass through five distinct climate zones.

23.) KULA BOTANICAL GARDENS
Mile Marker 8.5 – Highway 377 (★★★☆☆)

The King Protea is just one of the many flowers you can find in Kula Botanical Gardens. The King Protea has earned its way into the Mauʻi flowers hall of fame.

About half a mile beyond mile marker 8 you'll find our next stop on the left side of the road, Kula Botanical Gardens. Kula Botanical Gardens is home to nearly 2,000 species of indigenous Hawaiian floral and fauna.

The true king of this garden is the showy protea. However, the plants aren't the only thing to see at Kula Botanical Garden. There are also some great views from their reception center. A stream and koi pond can also be found in the six acres of the garden. It is open Monday-Saturday from 9am until 4pm. Admission is $5.

24.) POLIPOLI SPRINGS STATE PARK
Mile Marker 8.9 – Highway 377 (★★★☆☆)

Right before mile marker 9 on Highway 377, on the left, you'll see the turn off for Waipoli Road. Waipoli Road includes several switch backs up the side of Haleakala to Polipoli Springs State Park, an infrequently visited but very beautiful state park on Mau'i.

Polipoli Springs State Park is located around 6,200 feet above sea level in the Kula Forest Reserve and encompasses nearly ten-acres of recreational area. The upcountry park offers amazing views of both Mau'i below and the neighboring islands of Lana'i and Kaho'olawe. The towering trees, mature forest of redwoods, and other exotic native vegetation species such as plum, cypress, sugi, and ash are the highlights of the park. Several trails are also available.

Since the road is only partially paved, and the rest merely graded dirt and gravel, it is recommended mostly for 4-wheel drive vehicles. However the first part of the drive should be quite accessible and you can walk the rest of the way up if you're feeling up to a hiking challenge. A light jacket might also be a good idea as it can become quite chilly occasionally. If you decide to skip this stop, you'll soon find yourself back at the first junction of Highway 37/377.

HALEAKALA HIGHWAY

When you come to Mau'i, there is one thing above all others, literally, you simply cannot miss, Haleakala. The summit of this grand volcano rises 10,023 feet above sea level. The crater is 3,000 feet deep, 7.5 miles long and 2.5 miles wide - a total of 22 miles in circumference. Haleakala easily makes up the majority of the island of Mau'i. This section of our book is designed to introduce you to this amazing National Park and to educate you on the Haleakala Highway and Summit Area.

Historically speaking, Haleakala was originally part of the Hawai'i Volcanoes National Park, located on the Big Island of Hawai'i. On July 1, 1961, the park was re-designated as a separate entity. Later, Haleakala National Park was

This NASA satellite image gives a bird's eye view of the visitors center and giant crater basin waiting to be explored.

designated an International Biosphere Reserve in 1980. Of its 28,655 total acres, a whopping 19,270 acres remain complete wilderness. Haleakala National Park was originally established to preserve the outstanding features of Haleakala Crater and the Summit area. Later, additions to the park gave protection to the unique and fragile ecosystems and rare biotic species of the Kipahulu Valley, which includes the scenic pools along the 'Ohe'o Gulch (aka Seven Sacred Pools) and the local coastal area. Stretching from the summit of Mt. Haleakala eastward to the southeast coast, the park joins these two special areas - Haleakala Crater near the summit and the Kipahulu area on the coast beyond Hana Town. No roads connect the two, though each can be reached by different roads starting near Kahului.

Today, Haleakala is an active, but not currently erupting, volcano that last erupted roughly around 1790 near the coast. Over 200 years later, the land surrounding the lava flow area is still barren. Most lava flows in the crater actually took place around 900 years ago, which is really not that old geologically speaking. From Haleakala's summit you will experience one of the world's greatest views. Pu'u o Mau'i, the tallest cinder cone in the crater, is 900 feet tall from the

crater's floor; but you'd never guess it unless you take one of the many hikes into the crater. Haleakala National Park is open 24 hours a day and has an entrance fee of $10. This fee is good for both the summit and the Kipahulu area.

THE GEOLOGY OF HALEAKALA VOLCANO

Today, Haleakala Crater is a cool, cone-studded reminder of a once-active volcano. Streaks of red, yellow, gray and black trace the courses of recent and ancient lava, ash, and cinder flows. The volcanic rocks slowly break down as natural forces reduce them to minute particles, which are swept away by wind, heavy rain, and intermittent streams. This model (below) shows Haleakala as it exists today.

If we take a look at contemporary geology, it indicates that the Hawaiian Islands are situated near the middle of the "Pacific Plate." This Pacific Plate is almost always constantly moving northward at a rate of several centimeters per year, about the same rate as your fingernails grow. This constant northwestward movement of the Pacific Plate over a local volcanic "hot spot," or plume, has produced a series of islands, one after another in assembly line fashion. The result is a chain of volcanic islands stretching from the Big Island of Hawai'i along a southeast-northwest line for 2,500 miles toward Japan and the Aleutian Islands of Alaska. Mau'i, one of the younger islands in this chain, began as two separate

volcanoes on the ocean floor over a million years ago. As
the two volcanoes erupted time and time again, they created
thin new sheets of lava spread upon the old, building and
building until the volcanic heads emerged from the sea. First
the West Mauʻi Mountains formed as they sat over the ʻhot
spot' in the plate. But as the plate shifted, so did the location
of the rising magma, and thus Haleakala began its ascent,
eventually towering over its predecessors to the west. At its
greatest height, Haleakala likely reached some 14,000 feet
above the ocean – over some 30,000 feet from its base on
the ocean floor. That's taller than Mount Everest from top
to bottom. Lava, wind-blown ash, and alluvium eventually
joined the two volcanoes by an isthmus or valley, forming
Mauʻi, "The Valley Isle."

For a time, volcanic ac-
tivity ceased and ero-
sion dominated. The
great mountain was
high enough to trap
the moisture-laden
northeast trade winds.
Rain fell and streams
began to cut channels
down its slopes. Two

such streams began eroding their way inward creating large
amphitheater-like depressions near the summit. Ultimately,
these two valleys met, creating a long erosional "crater" that
nearly split the mountain in two.

When volcanic activity resumed near the summit, lava
poured down the stream valleys, nearly filling them. More
recently, cinders, ash, volcanic bombs, and spatter were
blown from numerous young vents in the "crater" forming
multicolored symmetrical cones as high as 900 feet, like

Pu'u o Mau'i. Thus the "crater" of Haleakala is really more of a volcanic crater basin than a true volcanic landform. It has partially filled with lava, crumbling rock, and cinder cones that you see today.

Several hundred years have passed since the last volcanic activity occurred within the crater. This stillness in Mau'i is instigated by the constant northwestward movement of the Pacific Plate. As the oldest islands on the northwest end of  the chain have moved farther away from the plume (source of new lava) they have ceased to grow. The ravages of wind and rain and time have thus been able to reduce them to sandbars and atolls. Mau'i has shifted a few miles from the plume's influence, and Haleakala too is destined to become extinct. Volcanic activity has since moved on to the Big Island of Hawai'i a few hundred miles to the southeast. Though dormant now, in approximately 1790, which is quite recent in geologic time, two minor flows at lower elevations along the southwest rift zone of Haleakala reached the sea and altered the southwest coastline of Mau'i.

Today, earthquake records indicate that internal adjustments are still taking place in the earth's crust at Haleakala, but at present, no volcanic activity of any form is visible. Perhaps Haleakala could erupt again; perhaps not. However, rest assured that your visit is safe.

HALEAKALA HIGHWAY

1.) STARTING POINT - HALEAKALA HWY
Junction of Hwy 377 & Hwy 378

The road to the Haleakala summit, known as the famous Haleakala Highway, holds the world record for climbing to the highest elevation in the shortest distance of 38 miles (Kahului to the Summit). The journey will take you along 32 switchbacks at an average grade of around six percent.

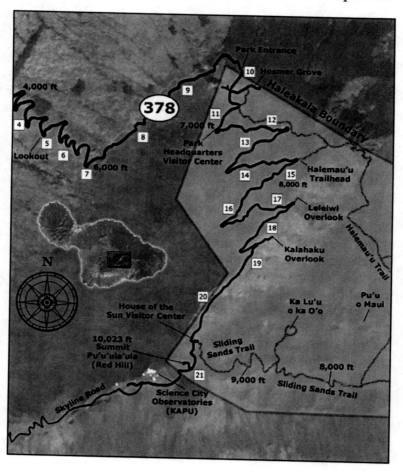

For every 1,000 feet you climb, the temperature will drop another three degrees Fahrenheit. The drive climbing through upcountry Mau'i to Haleakala's summit is one of the trip of a lifetime. There are three parts to the "Haleakala Highway" you should know about.

1.) The 'Lower Haleakala Highway' is the area between the two junctions of Highways 37 and 377 on Highway 37.

2.) The 'Upper Haleakala Highway' is the area between the two junctions of Highways 37 and 377 on Highway 377.

3.) The 'Haleakala Highway' then, as we refer to it, begins near Kahului along Highway 37 and continues into upcountry Mau'i onto Highway 377 and then turns onto Highway 378. Highway 378, also called Crater Road, is where the 21-mile journey to the summit begins.

Haleakala can be enjoyed on foot, bicycle, horseback, motorcycle, or car. From the base to the summit, Haleakala National Park ranges through five distinctly different climate zones, each with its own unique environment. Many guided hikes and tours offered by the National Park rangers and private activity companies. In this guide, we cover many of the hikes in enough detail that you can likely do them yourself. We'll also recommend the best ones to take. Haleakala National Park also offers a chance for visitors to get a look at the rare Silversword plant, unique only to Hawai'i. This is a threatened species of plant that only grows above 6,000 feet. The plant can live for up to 50 years and only blooms once before ending its lifecycle. And speaking of threatened species, keep your eyes open for the state bird of Hawai'i, the Hawaiian Goose or Nene (see page 91).

2.) HALEAKALA HIGHWAY LOOKOUTS
Mile Markers 5-9 - Highway 378 (★★★☆☆)

As you begin your journey, make sure to note the vegetation around you. If you do so now, you'll really appreciate just how much it's going to change on your trip up the mountain. The first seven miles of the highway are almost nothing but switchbacks, taking you from around 3,500 feet in elevation to over 6,000 feet.

Near mile 5 along these switchbacks we have our first stop. Here you will see a pull-off on the right side of the road for the initial lookout. Before you will be the island of Molokini (a popular snorkel haven) and uninhabited Kahoʻolawe, which only recently was turned back over to the state of Hawaiʻi from the US military.

If sea levels dropped, these islands would all be connected, and Molokini would look similar to modern Diamond Head on the nearby island of Oahu. If you look into the distance, on the right, you'll see the West Mauʻi Volcano remnants, all of which are much older than Haleakala. As we mentioned before, these two volcanoes joined together eons ago to form the single island of Mauʻi, with a valley (isthmus) between them. Hence why Mauʻi is dubbed the Valley Isle. Tucked behind the West Mauʻi mountains, on a clear day, you can likely locate the island of Lanaʻi. Lanaʻi would also be part of Mauʻi if sea levels were to drop. In fact, 20,000 years ago, during an ice age, the sea levels were 300 feet lower than they are today. At that time there was a landmass known as Mauʻi Nui (literally Big Mauʻi), which consisted of the islands of Lanaʻi, Molokaʻi, Kahoʻolawe, and present day Mauʻi.

On clear days, from around 6,000 feet, you can start to clearly make out the West Maui Mountains, wrapped in their usual cloud blanket, off in the distance.

As we continue on our journey, around mile marker 9.3 you'll notice the road has been cut through the earth. At this location, on your right, you get a good look at the inside of a cinder cone where the road slices through it. In ancient eruptions of Haleakala, cinders were thrown from the vent as hot and glowing, yet still solid fragments. As they fell around the vent they built up the cone you see today. The red and rusty hues are the result of iron-rich compounds essentially 'rusting' the black lava over the years.

HALEAKALA HIGHWAY

3.) HALEAKALA NATIONAL PARK ENTRANCE
Mile Marker 10 - Highway 378

You'll approach the official entrance to the park right beyond mile marker 10. Here you will see the official 'Haleakala' sign welcoming you to the park.

The $10 fee for admission is good for both the summit and Kipahulu area of the park. If you already paid in Kipahulu, just show them your park pass or receipt.

Welcome to the 'House of the Sun.' Haleakala National Park actually used to be part of Hawai'i Volcanoes National Park (on the Big Island), but was split off in 1960 as its own separate park unit. Today the park hosts between one and two million visitors annually, and since the park is open 24 hours a day, you can visit the summit any time you like, day or night. In fact, even between 3:00 am and 6:00 am, several hundred people can be found shivering as they wait for La (the sun) to rise.

HALEAKALA NATIONAL PARK FLORA & FAUNA

Haleakala is a gold mine of rare plants and wildlife. Below we'll introduce you to three of the many you'll find here.

The Silversword

There is only one place on the entire planet you'll find the silversword, Hawai'i. Believe it or not, the silversword is actually a member of the sunflower family.

The Nene

A distant relative of the Canada goose, the Nene has evolved and adapted to the harsh volcanic landscapes of Hawai'i. If you look closely at their feet you'll notice they've lost most of the webbing for rock gripping toes.

The Chukar

This partridge-like bird can be found near the summit of Haleakala. They are found only on a few select islands in the Hawaiian chain and are native to Asia and eastern Europe.

4.) HOSMER GROVE HIKE & SUPPLY TRAIL
Mile Marker 10 - Highway 378 (★★☆☆☆☆)

At approximately mile marker 10.5 you'll want to turn left to the start of the Hosmer Grove trail. At about 0.3 miles down the road (on the right) you may notice one of Hawai'i's famous sandalwood trees. The sandalwood has a long history in Hawai'i and was once very precious in China for incense and aromatic woodcarvings. In the 1800s the Pacific sailing-ship trade practically obliterated the Hawaiian sandalwood forests. Today you can still find sandalwood pits in Hawai'i where the trunks of the trees were stored. The pits were made to resemble the cargo areas of the ships the trees were transported in.

At this same location you'll also find our feature attraction for this stop, a half-mile-long nature trail that winds through a very intriguing forest of introduced trees not native to Hawai'i. It was back in 1910 that Ralph Hosmer planted this and other groves of trees like eucalyptus from Australia, sugi pine from Japan, deodar from India, Douglas fir and several species of pine from mainland United States, along with other species in hopes of introducing a timber industry as well as reestablishing the watershed. Today the grove presents the existing and continual dilemma of the struggle between native plants and introduced species in the Hawaiian Islands. The Haleakala Park Service labors intensively to make sure none of the non-native plants escape the grove, and the native vegetation in the surrounding continues to grow and thrive.

A lot of the trees are labeled on the short walk through the grove. Pick up a handy brochure at the beginning of the trail that will guide you along. As of this printing, there was a website we found that offered a trail map and small booklet (as noted above) available for printing. You can obtain the booklet by visiting the website at:

http://www.hear.org/usgs-brd-pierc-hfs/hosmergrove.htm

Our recommendation is that you visit Hosmer Grove quickly, perhaps doing a small portion of the hike, and then continue on your journey towards the summit. The best is still ahead of you at this point. Don't waste too much time at this spot.

The Supply Trail

While it is unlikely you'll want to even consider this challenging trail (because there are better and easier ones ahead in our opinion), we do want to mention it while we're here. The Supply Trail starts on the road that leads to Hosmer Grove and winds up through the native subalpine shrubland that dominates this elevation. Despite it's difficulty, this could be a good chance to closely observe the local plant and wildlife away from the road. The Supply Trail is fairly steeply graded from the start, but becomes even steeper as it approaches the connection with the Halemau'u Trail (page 95) at 3.5 miles in. You'll have park your car in the Hosmer Grove campground walk back along the road to the trailhead sign.

5.) PARK HEADQUARTERS VISITOR CENTER
Mile Marker 11 - Highway 378 (★★★★☆)

About one mile past the entrance you'll come to the Haleakala National Park Headquarters Building. This is a good place to stop and familiarize yourself with the park and browse the store inside. Anyone planning to hike into the crater and camp overnight needs to obtain a permit here (for camping only). The Park Headquarters building is at about 7,000 feet above sea level. At this altitude the clouds begin to come in thin in Hawai'i, as this elevation marks the top of the NE trade wind clouds.

It is at this elevation you will begin to notice just how quickly the environment changes as you go up. But climate is only one of the factors affecting the environment here. Livestock has been the other reason for the noticeable changes before you. Prior to the 1920s in Hawai'i, the Haleakala Ranch would drive their cattle up the slopes to the far boundaries of their ranch, which was then at the summit. Here the cows, and occasionally goats, would graze on the eastern crater wall disrupting the natural environment of the mountain. Today a mix of man-made fences and the help of hunters have restored Haleakala to a more natural state.

Hours: Park Headquarters 8:00AM - 4:00PM

6.) HALEMAU'U TRAIL HEAD (To Summit)
Mile Marker 14 - Highway 378 (★★★☆☆)

Continuing up the mountain, at approximately 14.2 miles into our journey, you'll see the parking lot for Halemau'u Trail. This rather long trail starts at 7,990 feet in the native shrub land ecosystem and leads down into the crater before traversing back up all the way to the summit of Haleakala. A hiker might choose to do a two mile round trip hike out to the edge of the valley and return, or might use this as a starting point for an all day hike to the summit. If you do choose the all day hike, we highly recommend you see our description and suggestions for this trail, located on page 109, because when doing the full day hike, it is better to start from near the summit.

If you do stop at this location, keep your eyes open for Nene (page 91). They are frequently spotted here. For their well-being, please do not feed them, even if they beg.

7.) LELEIWI OVERLOOK & HIKE
Mile Marker 17 - Highway 378 (★★★★★)

At mile 17.5 you'll want to pull into the parking lot on the right side of the road. Cross the road on foot and take the short 900 ft trail to the overlook for a panoramic view of the vast crater of Haleakala. Many folks don't even notice this location because at first glance, even along the trail, it appears nothing is here. Don't make that mistake! You'll notice that the view is very close to a more distant location, the moon. In fact, NASA has used this area for just that purpose. The astronauts that landed on the moon trained here.

This gigantic depression is 7.5 miles long (east to west); 2.5 miles wide, and 3,000 feet deep. This crater is so massive that the entire island of Manhattan could fit inside. From the lookout you could gaze at the rooftops of the skyscrapers.

You'd swear nothing was here until you hiked down the short trail. Then, suddenly, this scene pops into view before you.

Sometimes in the late afternoon, clouds stack up inside the crater and block the view from this location, but don't fret because you might be in for another treat. If this occurs and the sun is behind you, look into the cloudy mist directly away from the sun. You may be one of the lucky people who are able to see the phenomenon labeled as the 'Specter of the Brocken.' Native Hawaiians often will call it the Ho'okuaka, a view of the soul. Around your shadow in the mist will be a halo of rainbow colors. This same spectacle can sometimes be seen from an airplane window if you are looking down on a cloud top. An apparent rainbow encircles the shadow of the plane. This phenomenon is caused by the small spaces between the cloud droplets (diffraction) rather than by the bending of light rays within the droplets that form a rainbow (refraction).

Again, be sure to make note of how the vegetation has changed from near Park Headquarters at the 7,000 foot elevation. Where you once observed mostly low bushes and a sprinkling of lava, at nearly 2,000 feet higher the landscape has become mostly exposed lava and cinders with scarce

patches of vegetation in between. Low temperatures, high winds, thin air, and the sun's ultraviolet rays makes it difficult for many things to thrive here.

8.) KALAHAKU OVERLOOK & HIKE
Mile Marker 18 - Highway 378 (★★★★★)

At approximately mile marker 18.7, turn left onto a short road and drive to the parking area. The rim overlook, at 9,324 feet, provides another superb view of the crater floor. At one time, Haleakala likely resembled Mauna Loa on the Big Island with its pointed top. But as Haleakala's eruptions diminished and erosion in the early valleys of Keanae (Koʻolau Gap) on the north and Kaupo (on the south) began, they nearly almost merged together near the volcano's summit, splitting Haleakala in two.

There really is no precise historical record of Haleakala's most recent eruption, but an interesting piece of detective work sets it at about 1790. An explorer by the name of La Perouse mapped Mauʻi's shoreline in 1786. He drew a broad, shallow bay between two points on the southwest coast. Combined with another chart of the area, the fact that the peninsula lava flow looks very young, and local legend tells of eruptions at approximately that time, 1790 has since become the most logical date of the last eruption of Haleakala. The area south of the flow is now known as La Perouse Bay, in honor of the man who mapped it.

Now is the time to keep your eyes peeled for the spiky silversword. This unusual plant, unique to Haleakala, has thoroughly adapted to the harsh environment of its home. The bloom stalk is a true sight to behold, often several feet tall with a hundred or more purple flowers. What makes the blooming of a silversword even more special is that the plants live from 15 to more than 50 years but bloom only once and die. If you see one in bloom, take a moment to realize how unique that opportunity really is. In the not so distant past there were so many silverswords on

Haleakala they covered the ground like a blanket of snow, but because of livestock and visitors snapping portions for souvenirs, this amazing plant almost became extinct. In 1927, barely 100 plants were alive on the slopes of Haleakala. It was ultimately the creation of Haleakala National Park that saved the silversword. The protection and work of several dedicated groups have brought them back from that low in 1927 to more than 40,000 today. But even now, the silversword is at risk in its fragile environment, so please let these amazing plants live in peace. Don't touch or even walk near them, as you could damage their very delicate root structures.

9.) HOUSE OF THE SUN VISITOR CENTER
Mile Marker 20 - Highway 378 (★★★★★)

Around mile marker 20.5 you'll want to turn left at the intersection into the large parking lot for the House of the Sun visitor center. From the visitor center, you can catch the world's best view of Haleakala Crater. This tapestry of cinder cones, red banks, and lava flows took millions of years to form. The cinder cones provide a muted mixture of reds, oranges, and grays. Don't be fooled, the cinder cones may seem small from here, but they actually reach heights of over 600 ft high. To have full appreciation for the sheer size of these craters, you really have to hike among them. Once we reach the summit, we'll comment more on that. In geological terms the cinder cones and crater-floor flows that can be seen from this location are very young. During the last 2,500 years it is estimated that some 20 eruptions have likely taken place inside the crater. Today we can substantiate that number by taking into account that several lava flows inside the crater are not covered by red ash

deposits; deposits that are believed to have fallen about 2,500 years ago. Another clue to the ages of these cinder cones can be found by the fire goddess herself, Pele. A much less scientific method, for sure. For example, Pu'u o Pele

(Hill of Pele) is a cinder cone on the south floor of Haleakala Crater. Places in Hawaii that include the name of Pele typically imply that it was named post-Polynesian arrival in approximately 800 AD. Therefore, we can assume the volcanic activity that occurred at Pu'u o Pele has occurred since that time. Radiocarbon dating has since confirmed this conclusion in more recent years.

This location is also the start of the Sliding Sands Trail, something we highly recommend for those who want to do some nature loving. Make sure you put on sturdy shoes and a warm jacket as you prepare to hike into the crater. At first glance the smooth sand trail might seem like a piece of cake. But after a few switchbacks you'll realize the enormity and surreal silence of the crater. Make sure to turn around and observe the relative smallness of those hiking behind you. Volcanic ash and cinders can be thanked for the sand that covers this trail. Remember, at this altitude the air is thin. This means that while hiking down is a breeze, going back up is more of a challenge and may take twice as long. We recommend traveling to the first cinder cone, Ka Lu'u o Ka 'O'o, and then making the trip back for a good half-day hike. You can read more on this hike on page 106.

Hours: Visitor Center 7:30 am to 3:30 pm.

10.) HALEAKALA SUMMIT (PU'U 'ULA'ULA)
Mile Marker 21 - Highway 378 (★★★★★)

After leaving the visitor center you'll definitely want to head up to the summit. Turn left out of the visitor center parking lot and at mile marker 21 you'll come to another intersection. You'll want to take a right to reach the parking lot for the summit (the left road takes you to visit Science City and the observatories, but they are off limits to the public).

The summit parking lot is built in the shallow crater of Pu'u 'Ula'ula (Red Hill). Before you walk up the ramp to the summit look around you and observe some of Pele's fiery missiles. These chunks of lava were catapulted through the air during eruptions and hardened on their trip to the ground. The largest chunk is roughly four to five feet across. Pu'u 'Ula'ula is the highest point on Haleakala. Climb the steps to the shelter or take the more gradual ramp from the far end of the parking lot. If you look to the southeast you will probably see the high summits of Mauna Loa and Mauna Kea Volcanoes on the Big Island, each over 13,000 feet in elevation, poking their summits through the clouds.

Here, Haleakala's summit elevation is 10,023 feet, but the mountain was once much higher than this. A number of

factors have contributed to Haleakala's shrinking, including thousands of years of erosion, rapid caldera collapse, and slow island subsidence (sinking into the ocean bed). It can be concluded that the summit of Haleakala at one time in the distant past probably reached an elevation of 13,000 to 14,000 feet, higher than the modern day volcanoes on the Big Island.

As you look to the southwest, just outside the park on the next cinder cone of the rift, you will see Science City which you passed by earlier. Unfortunately, it is primarily off

limits to the public and none of the high altitude observatories allow visitors. Scientists use the observatories to track satellites, measure the wobble of the moon, and conduct other space research.

The summit of Haleakala is the altar of the sun. Many brave tourists choose to drive the highway in the wee hours of the morning in hopes of catching a Haleakala sunrise. However, many people are unprepared for what they find at the summit, bone–chilling cold and sometimes gusty winds. Some misguided tourists try to bear the 20–40 degree cold armed only with summer clothes and a hotel towel.

Those unfortunate shivering sunrise visitors can thank the demigod of Mau'i for the slow pace of the sun. As you may have noticed on the sign entering the park, Mau'i is snaring La, the sun god. He did so for his mother Hina, who needed more hours in the day for her tapa cloth to dry. Using twine, Mau'i snared La and made a deal with him to "walk" more slowly across the sky from that day on. See page xi for more details about the legend of the demigod Mau'i.

HALEAKALA HIGHWAY

HALEAKALA SUMMIT ACTIVITIES

If there is one thing Haleakala is not short of, beyond beauty, its activities. At first glance you might think that there's not a whole lot to do atop the mighty volcano. The sheer size of the mountain sometimes masks the adventures that can be found there. A few of the most popular are hiking (our favorite), bike riding, horseback riding, camping, viewing the sunrise/sunset, and observing rare species (flora/fauna) in their natural habitat. That might not sound like a lot, but believe us, it is. Over the following pages we'll go into detail on each of them, especially hiking, which we believe is the most rewarding experience you can have on Haleakala.

One popular "activity" on Haleakala is silversword hunting. It's cheating, but in the parking lot at the summit you can view these amazing plants up close. Look, but don't touch.

HIKING & TRAIL GUIDE

The summit of Haleakala has several trails that you'll want to make note. A trip to the top of Haleakala really isn't complete without embarking on at least one of these trails. If we had to pick just one, then hands down we'd go with the Sliding Sands Trail (page 106). On the following pages we'll cover the major hikes at the summit.

Pa Kaoao Trail
Haleakala Summit (★★★★☆)

This short trail (less than .5 mile round trip) leads to the top of Pa Kaoao, a small cinder cone. The trail offers one of the highest vantage points in the park and gives spectacular views of the wilderness of the volcano. Stone shelters built by the early Hawaiians that explored Haleakala long ago are still visible from the trail. The trail starts just outside of the House of the Sun Visitor Center at 9,740 feet.

Sliding Sands Trail
Haleakala Summit (★★★★★)

This trail is definitely not an easy hike, but it does come highly recommended as a good, if not the best, hike for the Haleakala summit area. The extremely strenuous trail descends 2,800 feet in the first 4 miles to the valley floor. The Keoneheehee (Sliding Sands) Trail starts at the bulletin board by the entrance to the Haleakala Visitor Center parking lot. For a good half-day (and yet still moderately strenuous) hike, we recommend the first 2.5 miles of the trail to the Ka Lu'u o ka O'o cinder cone (photograph on page 107) before turning around and taking the trail back out. The round trip is a 5-mile trek, and given the elevation, it'll feel like it's longer. The final climb back up Haleakala's Crater Rim will also be more than enough hike for one day.

The first two and a half miles along Sliding Sands trail will take you by ancient lava bombs, through a silversword colony, and around the rim of Ka Lu'u o ka O'o cinder cone.

If you want to have a full appreciation for the sheer size of Hale-akala's crater basin, then Sliding Sands trail will deliver it completely. When you begin the hike, take notice of Ka Lu'u o ka O'o below you in the crater (the one with the path around the rim). Compare that to the above image, on the rim itself. Wow!

For overnight trips, Keoneheehee Trail leads to Kapalaoa cabin in 5.6 miles, or Paliku cabin and campsite in 10.4 miles. On long treks to the central valley or beyond it is recommended that you hike the Halemau'u Trail out of the valley due to the steepness and soft cinder base of the Keoneheehee Trail.

Be sure you take water and necessities for hiking. Wear proper clothing (it can be cold at 10K+ feet) and make sure you are wearing sunscreen. We highly recommend a hiking pole of some sort as well, as it will make the climb back out of the crater much easier. Our final recommendation is that you prepare for this hike by getting a decent meal and good night's rest the day before. A bit of wisdom from those who have lived and learned, hiking this trail with too little energy from food and/or just a few hours of sleep can make it about 10 times harder than it needs to be.

Halemau'u Trail (Starting from the Summit)
Haleakala Summit (★★★☆☆)

This is a challenging, but rewarding 11.2-mile hike that traverses much of the Haleakala Wilderness. From this location, you are actually at the end of the trail because, as you likely noticed, the trailhead for Halemau'u was back at

mile marker 14. But we highly recommended that if you are going to hike the trail that you start from here instead of at the trailhead. Of course, you'll have to leave your vehicle at the trailhead and get a ride from another park visitor to the Haleakala Visitor Center near the summit. This way your car is waiting for you when you complete your journey, and trust us, you'll be glad it's there waiting for you. The trail starts from the House of the Sun Visitor Center parking lot as the Keoneheehee or Sliding Sands Trail. The trail descends 2,500 feet in 3.9 miles to the valley floor. At this point the trail splits and a hiker on this route would take the left fork off of Keoneheehee Trail onto a spur trail where signs lead toward Holua. This spur trail travels up past colorful cinder cones and varied terrain. From Holua, travel approximately one mile across a grassland area to the base of a 1,000 foot cliff. After hiking up two miles of switchbacks the trail levels off and continues one more mile to the Halemau'u Trailhead and parking lot. The average time to complete this route is 6-8 hours. Get an early start so you can get the most out of your hike and make it back to your car before nightfall.

Trail Information Source: National Park Service

HALEAKALA HIGHWAY

BIKE RIDING
Haleakala Summit to Upcountry (★★★☆☆)

One of the most popular activities on Haleakala is bike riding. At first thought this might sound a bit odd, especially for those who are thinking, "I know I just read this is the steepest climbing road in the world somewhere..." Don't worry, the only way to ride a bike on Haleakala is down. Starting at the summit each morning the vans line up to bring hundreds to the top of Haleakala, some early enough to even watch the sunrise. Then, dressed in their warmest jackets, gloves, and pants, they jump on their specially made bikes (extra padded brakes) and make the journey down the mountain some 38 miles to the ocean, shedding the layers of clothing as they go. Some say it's the most rewarding activity found on Mau'i, and that's probably why some 70,000 folks a year make the ride down Haleakala's slope.

Now some words of caution. First, this activity can be costly and can also be hazardous. Traveling down the world's steepest road (distance wise) in traffic and without many barriers on the side of the road isn't classified as the safest activity on Mau'i. You can expect to get up very early, 2 am-3 am at the latest. Then you'll ride in a van, sometimes a cramped van, with 20 other folks to the top of the mountain. You'll want to dress very warmly, as most people will under dress severely and freeze there you-know-what off, especially once they get moving down the mountain on a bike in the cold morning air at 20mph (the van companies will advise you to move at this speed; it is faster than it sounds on a bike.)

With that said, it's really up to you to decide if this activity is for you. There are just as many who will call it overrated as there are who will say it's the best thing they've done on Mau'i. So definitely do your homework and make sure you know about all the perks and risks equally.

HORSE BACK RIDING (INTO THE CRATER)
Haleakala Summit (★★★★☆)

Another popular, yet pricey, activity on Haleakala is a horseback ride into the crater. For those who aren't up to hiking down Sliding Sands Trail into the basin and still want to see the cinder cones inside the volcano, this may be for you. As of press time, there was one company that we know of that provides these tours, Pony Express. They provide visitors with a ride down Sliding Sands Trail to the bottom of the crater. They only take approximately eight people a day, so you'll need to make your reservations far in advance (2-3 weeks minimum). The cost of a ride (as of this printing) was $155 for four hours, and $190 to Kapalaoa Cabin at 12 miles into the crater.

Horseback is an easy way to see Haleakala from the inside. If you enjoy horseback riding, then this is definitely an activity for you.

HALEAKALA SUNRISE INFORMATION
Haleakala Summit (★★★★★)

If you're an early riser, you too can see why this volcano is called "House of the Sun." Each morning dozens of people flock to the summit of Haleakala to witness the sunrise above the 10,000 foot summit. If you want to beat the traffic and get a good spot, we suggest you leave no later than 3:30 am. As we mentioned previously, attempting to view the sunrise and hike in the same day are ill advised. When you get up at 3:30 am, your energy drains quickly at this elevation in the cold from shivering.

It takes one hour to reach the summit when leaving from Kahului, 1-½ hours from Kihei, and 2 hours from Lahaina. But despite the early morning rise, it's always well worth it. If you feel this is too early for you, consider a Haleakala sunset, but be aware more clouds are present later in the day. The very latest we'd suggest entering the park in the morning is 4:30 am, as sunrise will typically be around 5:30-6:30 am. Temperatures range between 20-40 degrees Fahrenheit at the summit of Haleakala, so be sure to dress warmly. A view of the sunrise is weather permitting, so check the weather before you go.

If you want to check the sunrise time of a specific day, check the solar chart at the following URL:
http://www.nps.gov/hale/pages/tier_three/sunrise_set.htm

M A U I
Mile by Mile

Waiheʻe Ridge Trail in north west Mauʻi is absolutely gorgeous heading inland. It's not until you start back you realize that the view behind you the whole time was also just as amazing.

Molokini island, off the south shore of Mauʻi, offers some of the best snorkeling in Hawaiʻi.

OTHER 'MUST SEE & DO' OF MAU'I

While the three drive guides we've covered already will surely be enough to please even the most demanding vacationers, we should note that there is a lot more to Mau'i than just what we cover in our guide. Our book is designed to primarily focus on the three major drives through east Mau'i, and hopefully it will aid you in experiencing all there is to see and do in this amazing part of the island. But since we like to be as thorough as possible, we want to at least briefly cover a few other 'Must See & Do' of Mau'i. Here's a few places we feel are deserving of a visit and we'll highlight them in the order they appear below:

La Perouse Bay, Makena (Big) Beach, 'Iao Valley & Needle, Dragon's Teeth, Kahekili Beach, Lahaina Town, Waihe'e Ridge & Valley, and Nakalele Blowhole.

Makena Beach is considered by many to be "the beach" on Mau'i.

LA PEROUSE BAY
Mile Marker 7 - Makena Alanui Road (★★★★☆)

Haleakala's last display can be seen on Mauʻi's southeast shore at La Perouse Bay. Scientists estimate that in 1790 Haleakala erupted to form the jagged lava rock coastline. Now there is a monument and ruins of Hawaiian natives who made their home on the sharp aʻa lava rock.

La Perouse is the end of the road, literally, in south Mauʻi. It is located at mile marker 7 at the very end of Makena Alanui Road. From Kihei take Piʻilani Hwy south to Wailea. Turn right on Wailea Iki road and bear left on to Wailea Alanui Road which turns into Makena Alanui. Look carefully around you as you drive between mile markers 5.5 and 7. On either side you should see fields of aʻa littering the landscape. Just past mile marker 6.5 look mauka (mountain side) and you can see where the lava spewed forth from Kalua o Lapa cinder cone.

Once you reach La Perouse Bay you may have to park on the road. Make sure not to park on any lava rock as it can ruin your day with a flat tire. (Trust us we know.)

You can walk through the lava and explore the sea estuaries. This is a favorite place for dolphins and local fishermen. Make sure to wear sunscreen and be prepared for a lot of wind.

MAKENA BEACH (BIG BEACH)
Mile Marker 4 - Makena Alanui Road (★★★★★)

Makena is probably one of the prettiest beaches on Mauʻi, certainly south Mauʻi. It is nearly 2/3 mile long and over 100 feet wide. The gorgeous sand and pristine waters attract snorkelers, swimmers and sunbathers. As with most beaches on Mauʻi, pay attention to the rip tides. Enter the water where the locals are; they know what they are doing. You can also get great views of Molokini and Kahoʻolawe. If you look to your right you will notice a large hill. This is 360-foot Puʻu Olaʻi, the legendary spot of a violent eruption before the one in 1790. Because of its location near the ocean, the pressure from the cool water and hot flowing lava built up massive pressure, resulting in a powerful explosion that propelled lava high into the air. The lava eventually fell and formed Puʻu Olaʻi. Porta potties and picnic tables are available. Makena Beach is accessible via a short road at mile marker 4 on Makena Alanui Road and another access just past mile marker 4.

'IAO VALLEY & NEEDLE
Mile Marker 2 - Highway 320 (★★★★★)

The 'Iao Needle is a major attraction nestled in the 'Iao Valley of the West Mau'i Mountains. It is a large tower-like formation, rumored to be the phallic symbol of Hawaiian god, Kanaloa. From the platform near the needle you can get several good photographs, but don't forget to turn around and catch a beautiful view of the ocean and central Mau'i. This was once the site of a bloody battle between King Kamehameha and the people of Mau'i. King Kamehameha slaughtered so many Hawaiians that the bodies clogged the stream until it ran red with blood. Today it is a tranquil and well-landscaped area with plenty of walking paths. Don't expect a lot of sunshine. The West Mau'i Mountains are rain magnets.

To get to the 'Iao Needle take Highway 32 west out of Kahului toward Wailuku. Take 32 through Wailuku until it turns into Highway 320. Follow the signs to the parking lot.

DRAGON'S TEETH
Mile Marker 30.5 - Off Honoapi'ilani Hwy (★★★★☆)

Dragon's Teeth is a good example of what can happen when forces of nature collide. As the lava from the West Mau'i Volcano poured into the ocean, fierce wind and waves forced it back and it cooled into a formation that resembles great black teeth. Honu (sea turtles) often swim close to shore, so peer over the edge and look for them. To get to Dragon's Teeth take Honoapi'ilani Hwy northeast and turn left onto Office Road just past mile marker 30. At the end of Office Road take a right and park in the little parking lot. You'll have to walk across the edge of a golf course to reach the teeth. As you walk, look to your right for a small plaque. This site is an ancient Hawaiian burial ground that was the subject of a huge controversy. The Ritz Carlton Hotel wanted the land for a beach front resort. They even began construction of the land before the Hawaiian community stepped in and put an end to it.

KAHEKILI BEACH
Mile Marker 25 - Honoapi'ilani Hwy (★★★★☆)

This beach is a nice little stop along the drive around West Mau'i. The park is dedicated to Kahekili, the last king of Mau'i before Kamehameha united the islands. Captain Cook noted Kahekili's fearsome tattoos that nearly covered one side of his body. Kamehameha fought very hard to defeat Kahekili, only to find out later that the Mau'i king was his father.

The tall palms, white sand and up close views of Molokai and Lana'i make it a perfect sunset spot. It is also a good

snorkeling place. Facilities are available, including picnic tables. To get there, turn left off Honoapi'ilani Hwy on to Kai Ala Dr. just after mile marker 25. There is a parking lot which closes shortly after sunset.

LAHAINA TOWN
Mile Marker 19.5 - Honoapiʻilani Hwy (★★★★☆)

You simply can't leave Mauʻi without experiencing Lahaina. A port town, Lahaina is full of things to see and do from shopping to exploring several historical sites. The main drag is Front Street which you can get to by turning left just before mile marker 20 on Honoapiʻilani Hwy. A few things to see in Lahaina are: the gigantic banyan tree which literally takes up an entire city block, the historic Baldwin House, the old courthouse, and the old prison. Be prepared to search and possibly pay for parking in Lahaina. It is incredibly popular and has the reputation for being crowded. There is plenty of shopping, dining and entertainment here. It is home to shows such as ʻUlalena and the Old Lahaina Luau.

Looking down Front Street in Lahaina, this is where vacationers come to have fun. No surprise there, as Lahaina was once the 'playground' of the aliʻi (royalty) when it was Hawaiʻi's capital.

M A U I
Mile by Mile

WAIHE'E RIDGE TRAIL & VALLEY
Mile Marker 6 - Highway 340 (★★★★★)

Have you ever wanted to stand at the top of a mountain in utter silence and commune with the clouds? That is exactly what you'll be able to do on the Waihe'e Ridge Trail. The 5-mile round trip trail ascends 1,500 feet through a lush forest of kukui, guava, ohi'a, and ferns. The earlier you start the trail the better chance you have of viewing the Waihe'e Valley without clouds. When you arrive at the trailhead it may not seem like much of a trail. You have to pass through a cattle-proof gate and up a 200-ft cement road that is far steeper than it looks. Just after half a mile, glance to your left and you'll be treated to Makamaka'ole Falls. There are a few other falls to see on the trail but most of them are far away and buried in the green draped

After huffing and puffing up the initial incline and a short walk through the forest this is your first reward - Waihe'e Valley.

The brilliant red and unique shape of the Ohi'a flower make it a delight to see, but red isn't the only color of this beautiful flower. It also comes in shades of white and yellow. Native birds love them for their nectar and can frequently be spotted nearby.

valleys of the West Mau'i Mountains. The trail goes in cycles of flat and steep areas culminating in a series of switchbacks that lead to the end, a hill called Lani-ili. At 2,563 feet you may be blessed with a clear view of the valley or you may be treated to a sea of clouds. Either way this is certainly a priceless experience.

To reach the trailhead, take Highway 32 west out of Kahului until you reach Highway 330, about three miles. Turn right on Highway 330 and continue until it becomes Highway 340 at mile marker 2. At 9/10 mile past mile marker 6 is the Maluhia Boy Scout Camp on the left. Turn left on to this road and it is approximately 1 mile up hill until you reach a small parking area.

M A U I
Mile by Mile

NAKALELE BLOWHOLE
Mile Marker 38.5 - Honoapiʻilani Hwy (★★★★☆)

When high tide and high surf combine you are likely to witness an explosive show from the Nakalele Blowhole. This phenomenon is caused by the ocean undercutting the shore and forcing seawater up through a large hole in the lava shelf. The blowhole is variable with the tide and surf, high tide is best. It is 1,200 feet from the road down an incline. There is a turnout about 1/2 mile past mile marker 38. You can see the blowhole from this spot but you must follow a trail down approximately 200 feet to reach it. Make sure you wear good sandals because there is some rock-skipping involved. Remember, it *is* possible to take a trip down the blowhole should you get too close. Use common sense and enjoy the show.

Visit the Nakalele blowhole when the tide is up and you're sure to get a blast, literally. Just don't get too close, because as fascinating as it appears, the forces at work are simply unreal.

END NOTES

Mauʻi no ka oi (Mauʻi is the best) – could any phrase be more fitting for the island of Mauʻi? By now, either through experience or by reading our guidebook, you likely will agree Mauʻi is a very amazing place to visit.

Whether your visit is your first or your twenty-first, Mauʻi is always sure to please those from all walks of life. The valley isle is full of adventures, beauty, discoveries, aloha, and even some ancient mysticism. Mauʻi is a place many mistakenly believe they will visit, enjoy, and then leave. What they don't realize is that Mauʻi's magic becomes part of you once you visit, and even when you leave, it comes along and stays with you forever.

We don't claim to be native Hawaiians; we're not. In fact, we're haole by birth, and we're not ashamed of that. We remain as true to our physical lineage as the native people of Hawai'i do to their own. But inside of ourselves we cannot question the impact of Mau'i upon us. Perhaps it is the blood of Native Americans that runs through our veins, or perhaps it's a familiar world only to our souls, nostalgic

for some ancient home we've spiritually experienced. As physically foreign as we are in Mau'i, we are spiritually at home all the same. In some sense, all the people of Hawai'i are visitors and guests in an enchanted land filled with more knowledge than a person could learn in ten lifetimes. Even the indigenous Hawaiians are descendents of Polynesian explorers from sometime around 800 AD. It was here, in the most isolated place on the earth that Hawai'i invoked their souls as well. The 'earth' spoke, and they listened – a system of life was born that remains famous for its chanting, mele (song), hula, language, kapu system, and more. You can visit Mau'i to vacation, but you'll leave with a greater appreciation for life, the aina (land), and the world as you know it. Stories abound the world over about the enlightening effects Mau'i has on an individual.

Mau'i is an island that is quite possibly as diverse as the planet itself. Almost all races of man can be found living on her volcanic lands. Mau'i has become a gathering point and melting pot of the world's cultures. And as many men flock here to create some commonality of the human race, the rarity of the fauna and flora species that thrive here are unique to all the world. Also, there are few landscapes or environmental conditions that cannot be found somewhere on Mau'i's shores. For every visitor, Mau'i offers something unique. From the richest person who desires first class luxury to the soul-searcher looking for deeper meaning, Mau'i is the answer. Despite who you are when you come to Mau'i, you will leave a changed individual. Mau'i has a way of creeping into your being, invoking your soul, and

The famous Banyan Tree on the Pipiwai Trail in Kipahulu.

M A U I
Mile by Mile

Lava fields at La Perouse are the youngest aina (land) on Mau'i.

rejuvenating the drive for life inside of you. Ironically so many choose to ignore this feeling upon their return home, misjudging it as mere wistfulness for a vacation they enjoyed some time in their past. This feeling, this calling, is actually 'Aloha' in its purest form, and if you kindle it inside of you, it will grow - then you too will know the magic of Mau'i.

Remember... Mau'i is both sacred and pure, born from the fiery depths of the earth by a goddess the Hawaiians call Pele. Do not mistake these people as purely mystical and full of senseless lore. A wise man once said to the missionaries of the 1800s,

> "Pele is the volcano, and the volcano is Pele... they are one in the same."

Do not take Pele's children (the rocks) from this land, and do not leave anything behind that you take into the wilderness. Respect the people, the aina, the kai (ocean), and yourself for who and what they are. Let your troubles go, and leave the world you left back home behind. Let your problems dissolve in this majestic place. And when you leave this beautiful island and the sensation creeps over you that you deem certain to be Aloha, let it grow inside of you.

Then you too will have found the magic of Mau'i, the beauty of these isles. Mau'i no ka oi - Mau'i is calling you back home. Will you answer the call?

Aloha & A Hui Hou,

John & Natasha Derrick

The authors, John & Natasha Derrick, at Wailua Falls.

BIBLIOGRAPHY, CREDITS, & STATEMENTS

Aerial Photographs
National Aeronautics and Space Administration (NASA)
<http://www.nasa.gov/>

Haleakala Art (Mauʻi snares the sun)
National Park Service (Haleakala NP entrance sign)

Mauʻi Trails – Walks, Strolls, and Treks on the Valley Isle;
Morey K. – Wilderness Press Berkeley: 2000

National Park Service; 2004-Oct
<http://www.nps.gov/hale/pages/tier_two/trails_kipahulu.htm>

Page Makers LLC; 2004-Oct
<http://www.haleakala.national-park.com/info.htm>

Road Guide to Haleakala and the Hana Highway;
Decker, Barbara & Robert. – Double Decker Press: 1992

— — — — — — — — — — —

Pony Express Tours
The Haleakala Horseback riding tour listing is not an advertisement for 'Pony Express Tours.' This listing is posted as a result of their services being the only known for this activity. Hawaiian Style Organization LLC is in no way affiliated with Pony Express Tours.

General Sight-Seeing
There are many locations on Mauʻi that are private property and we, to our best efforts, have attempted to avoid the use of such properties. It is our recommendation that all of our guide book readers avoid trespassing on Mauʻi when lands are clearly posted. Hawaiian Style Organization LLC takes no responsibility for the actions of its readers.

Dangers & Hazards
Mauʻi's paradise, make no mistake about it, but even paradise has its fair share of hazards. A few you should know about, in brief, are: Streams - don't underestimate the power of the streams/rivers in Hawaiʻi. One good rain, even far inland from where you are, can cause a stream to rise substantially. If you're crossing any streams or rock hopping, pay close attention to the weather and the water levels. The sun - A UV index of near 14+ every day speaks for itself. We recommend at least 15+ sunblock in Hawaiʻi at all times. Ocean life, plants, and animals - they're wild here too, so make sure you have respect for mother nature's creatures. There are a lot of plants and fruits you can eat alongside many trails in Hawaiʻi. Just make sure you've done your homework before biting into any mystery fruit. The ocean life and animals speak for themselves, don't become a statistic, be smart around wildlife.

Index

Symbols

7 Sacred Pools
    See Ohe'o Gulch

A

Airport
    Hana Airport 37
    Kahului Airport v, vii, 4
Alau Island 49, 50-51
Alelele Falls **68**

B

Beyond Hana
        Drive **45-80**
Big Island 33, 81, 85, 90, 100, 102, 103
Black sand beach 20, 40, 41, 47
Blue Angel Falls **39**
    Blue Pool 39

C

Central Mau'i v
Charles Lindbergh Grave **64-65**
    See also Palapala Ho'omau Church
Ching's pond **27**
Chukar 91
Crater Road **78**, 87
    See also Haleakala Highway

D

Demigod (Mau'i) xi-xiii
Dragons Teeth **119**

E

East Mau'i **vii**
Enchanting Floral Gardens **76**

G

Garden of Eden vii, **12-13**, 14, 15

H

Haipua'ena Falls **16**
Haleakala National Park vi, 58, 59, 68,
    70, 75, 77, 78, 80, **81-113**
    Bike riding 110-111
    Entrance **90**
    Hiking 105
    Horseback Riding 112
    Kipahulu Area **58**
    Park Headquarters 94
    Summit 102-103
    Summit Visitor Center 100
    Sunrise 113
Haleakala Highway
    Drive **81-113**
    Lower Haleakala Highway 75, 87
    Upper Haleakala Highway 77, 78, 87
Halemau'u Trail 93, **95**, 108, **109**
Hamoa Beach 49, **52-53**
Hana Bay 42, 47
Hana Highway
    See Road to Hana, Highway 360
Hana Town **42, 47**
Hanawi Falls **34**
Haneo'o Road **49**, 50-53
Hawaiian Goose
    See Nene
'Highway 36' 4-6
'Highway 360' 6
    See also Road to Hana
'Highway 365' 4

'Highway 37' 4, 75, 77
　See also Haleakala Highway, Lower
　Haleakala Highway
'Highway 377' 75, 77-80, 86, 87
　See also Haleakala Highway, Upper
　Haleakala Highway
'Highway 378' 78, 86, 87
　See also Haleakala Highway, Crater
　Road
Ho'okipa Beach 4, **5**
Honokowai iii
Honomanu Bay
　Honomanu Bay Road **20**
　Lookout **18, 21**
Hosmer Grove **92-93**

I
'Iao Valley 118
　'Iao Needle **118**

J
Jurassic Park Rock vii, 12

K
Ka'anapali iii
Kahana iii
Kahanu Garden **38**
Kahekili Beach 120
Kaho'olawe 74, 77, 117
Kahului 87, 113, 118, 123
Kalahaku Overlook **98**
Kapalua iii
Kaumahina State Wayside Park **17**
Kaupo Gap xiii, 70
Kaupo Store 69
Keanae
　Keanae Arboretum 8, **24-25**, 26
　Keanae Peninsula 17, 18, 22, **26**, 28

Keanae Peninsula Lookout **28**
Keoneheehee Trail **106-108**, 109
　See also Sliding Sands Trail
Kihei iv
Kipahulu viii, 58, 60, 65, 82, 90, 125
　See also Ohe'o Gulch
Koki Beach 49, **50-51**
Ko'olau Gap 29, 100
Kula Botanical Gardens **79**

L
Lahaina iii, **121**
Lana'i 74, 77, 88, 118
La Perouse Bay iv, 101, **116**
Lava Caves 33, 41
Leleiwi Overlook **96**
Lower Haleakala Highway
　See 'Highway 37'

M
Ma'alaea iv
Makahiku Falls **62**
Makapipi Falls **35**
Makena iv
Makena Beach **117**
Maps
　Beyond Hana 46, 49
　　Haneo'o Road 49
　　Upcountry Mau'i 75
　Haleakala 86
　Road to Hana 3, 31
　　Puohokamoa Falls 14
　Upcountry Mau'i 75
Mokulau 69
Molokai ii, 120

N

Nahiku
 Nahiku Landing 37
 Nahiku Road 36
Nakalele Blowhole 124
Napili iii
Nene 87, **91**, 95
Niihau ii
Nua'ailua Bay **23**

O

Ohe'o Gulch **58-63**, 82
 See also Pipiwai Trail, Waikmoku Falls,
 Makahiku Falls

P

Pa'ia town **4**
Painted Bark Eucalyptus 8, 24
Palapala Ho'omau Church 64-65
 See also Charles Lindbergh Grave
Pi'ilanihale Heiau **38**
 See also Kahanu Garden
Pipiwai Trail 44, 60, **61-63**, 127
Pokowai Sea Arch **71**
Polipoli Springs State Park **80**
Pua'a Ka'a State Wayside Park **32**
Punalau Falls **19**
Puohokamoa Falls 13
 Lower Puohokamoa Falls **15**
 Upper Puohokamoa Falls **14**

R

Rainforest 9-11
Region(s) iii
 See also Central Mau'i, East Mau'i,
 South Mau'i, Upcountry Mau'i, West
 Mau'i
Road to Hana
 Drive **1-43**

S

Sapphire blue pools
 See Ching's Pond
Sea Arch 40, 50, 71
Seven Sacred Pools
 See Ohe'o Gulch
Silversword 87, **91**, 99, 104, 106
Sliding Sands **106-108**, 109, 112
 See also Keoneheehee Trail
South Mau'i **iv**
Sun Yat-Sen Park **74**, 77
Supply Trail 93
 See also Hosmer Grove
Swimming 7, 27, 40, 51, 52, 54

T

Taro 24, 25
Tedeschi Winery 73
Three Bears Falls
 See Waikani Falls
Twin Falls **7**

U

Ula'ino Road 37, 38, 39
Upcountry **vi**, 73, 80, 87
Upper Haleakala Highway
 See 'Highway 377'

V

Venus Pool **54-55**

W

Wai'anapanapa State Park **40-41**
Waihe'e Ridge Trail 114, **122-123**
Waikamoi
    Waikamoi Forest 9
    Waikamoi Trail **9-11**
Waikani Falls
    Upper Waikani Falls **30**
Waikoa Pond
    See Venus Pool
Wailea iv
Wailua Falls **56-57**, 127
Wailua Valley State Wayside Park **29**
Waimoku Falls 60, 61, **62-63**
Waipoli Road 80
West Mau'i **iii**, 5, 59, 77, 119, 120, 122-123
West Mau'i Mountains i, ii, 73, 74, 84, 89, 118, 122-123

Discover more of Hawai'i
Mile by Mile

on *Kauai*

KAUAI - Mile by Mile Guidebook
1st edition

155 photos, 11 driving maps,
228 pages, detailed index, 5.25"x8.0"

Includes details on Hawaiian culture,
ecology, history, and more.

ISBN: 0-9773880-4-2 (Bound)
ISBN: 0-9773880-8-5 (eBook)

www.HawaiianStyleMedia.com

...Or
these amazing color products:

11x17"
photographic
prints,

15x19"
framed
pictures,

or 23x35"
posters!!

THE ISLAND OF MAUI HAWAII

Available only at:
www.HawaiianStylePhotos.com

20238